ASP.NET MVC 4 and the Web API

Building a REST Service from Start to Finish

D1473108

Jamie Kurtz

Apress

ASP.NET MVC 4 and the Web API

ISBN-13 (pbk): 978-1-4302-4977-1

ISBN-13 (electronic): 978-1-4302-4978-8

President and Publisher: Paul Manning
Lead Editor: Ewan Buckingham
Development Editor: Matthew Moodie
Technical Reviewer: Jeff Sanders
Editorial Board: Steve Anglin, Mark Beckner, Ewan Buckingham, Gary Cornell, Louise Corrigan, Morgan Ertel, Jonathan Gennick, Jonathan Hassell, Robert Hutchinson, Michelle Lowman, James Markham, Matthew Moodie, Jeff Olson, Jeffrey Pepper, Douglas Pundick, Ben Renow-Clarke, Dominic Shakeshaft, Gwenan Spearing, Matt Wade, Tom Welsh
Coordinating Editor: Jill Balzano
Copy Editor: Patrick Meader
Compositor: SPi Global
Indexer: SPi Global
Artist: SPi Global
Cover Designer: Anna Ishchenko

Distributed to the book trade worldwide by Springer Science+Business Media New York, 233 Spring Street, 6th Floor, New York, NY 10013. Phone 1-800-SPRINGER, fax (201) 348-4505, e-mail orders-ny@springer-sbm.com, or visit www.springeronline.com. Apress Media, LLC is a California LLC and the sole member (owner) is Springer Science + Business Media Finance Inc (SSBM Finance Inc). SSBM Finance Inc is a Delaware corporation.

For information on translations, please e-mail rights@apress.com, or visit www.apress.com.

Apress and friends of ED books may be purchased in bulk for academic, corporate, or promotional use. eBook versions and licenses are also available for most titles. For more information, reference our Special Bulk Sales–eBook Licensing web page at www.apress.com/bulk-sales.

Any source code or other supplementary materials referenced by the author in this text is available to readers at www.apress.com. For detailed information about how to locate your book's source code, go to www.apress.com/source-code/.

Dedicated to my wife, Kim. After nearly two decades together, she still manages to leave me speechless with her love, joy, peace, patience, kindness, goodness, faithfulness, gentleness, and self-control. Even as my work on this book has been fun and challenging, I know it is but an infinitesimal drop in the bucket of all that life has brought and will continue to bring us.

Contents at a Glance

Contents

Foreword

The site went live a month ago. There have been a few minor problems along the way, but for the most part things have gone smoothly... until today. End-of-month batch processing began about eighteen hours ago, and it isn't going well. We have less than six hours to finish generating the export files that we need to deliver to the credit card statement print vendor, and it doesn't look as though we're going to make it. Something is wrong with the interest calculations; they are taking way too long. Even worse, the calculations are incorrect for some of the Platinum accounts!

Another two hours pass. In the meantime, we, with the help of our lead business analyst, have found and fixed the problem with the interest calculation. However, the number of accounts processed per minute is noticeably declining. There's no way we're going to make the deadline at this rate. And if we don't deliver the goods, this whole over-budget project is in serious jeopardy.

The project manager calls the architect and some of us senior developers to his office and asks us how it's going—as if the answer to that question isn't obvious enough. So he says, "What about that new guy down in IT? Do you think he can help with this problem?"

Hmmm, we hadn't thought of asking him. After all, he wasn't part of the project, and it would take him way too long to come up to speed. Or would it? We don't have much to lose. Besides, we have been having him assist us with some of our more puzzling database and networking questions (which have seemed completely elementary to him), so we know he is a smart guy.

We hurry over to the IT department and find The New Guy surrounded by monitors, computer parts, books, and lots of empty Mountain Dew cans. He appears to already be aware of our problem (I suspect our manager has given him a heads-up). Our dashboard page is up on one monitor, and on the other monitors we see SQL Server Query Analyzer and some unfamiliar profiling tools. For the next hour or so, he hits us with a barrage of questions, rifles through our source code, and bangs away at the various diagnostic tools he has up on his screens. He's indexing tables, modifying stored procedures, and doing all sorts of other crazy stuff on—you got it—the live system. But it seems to be working, in a BIG way. The account processing rate has jumped by orders of magnitude. We're actually going to make the deadline!

That "New Guy" is from nearly a decade ago, and he represents my earliest memory of Jamie Kurtz. In the intervening years I, and many others, have grown to know him as wonder-geek, boss, and friend. For as long as I've known him, he has consistently been the go-to guy for the most baffling technology questions. He's always ready to grab the keyboard with a brusque, "Here, let me drive!" when he sees someone floundering. The depth of his knowledge, from architecture patterns to the arcane details of database server tuning, is astounding.

Think of this book as your chance to sit down with Jamie and have him show you what ASP.NET MVC 4 with Web API is, as well as how you can use it to solve real-world business problems. Jamie begins gently with a practical explanation of the HTTP protocol and REST, and then proceeds to walk you through the process of developing a task-management service, one that adheres to the tenets of the REST architecture and fully leverages the key capabilities available within the HTTP protocol.

But this isn't the typical "pop-technology" book that focuses exclusively on the technology without providing any sense of context. This book doesn't gloss over important details, propagate anti-patterns (e.g., how many books have you read with code-behind in the view classes?), or expect you to simply follow along like a little code monkey. The site that you and Jamie develop will be built upon solid software and database design patterns and principles, and it will incorporate best-of-breed supporting technologies (e.g., log4net and NHibernate) with painstakingly detailed explanations of the what, why, and how.

It's been a LONG time since I've learned so much from, and actually enjoyed, a technology book. I trust you will have a similar experience. Godspeed!

Brian Wortman
Fusion Alliance, Inc.
Indianapolis, IN
December, 2012

About the Author

Jamie Kurtz has more than 15 years of experience working in both development and production capacities on the Microsoft platform. While working as a developer and tester for an education-software company and as a developer in a high-temperature super conductivity lab, he received his Bachelor of Science from Western Michigan University. Jamie double majored in Physics and Mathematics and minored in Computer Science.

Since then, Jamie worked in DBA, project lead, team lead, manager, architect, tester, and developer roles in various industries, including: telecommunications, fulfillment, manufacturing, banking, and video intelligence/security. He is currently working as a consultant and group manager at Fusion Alliance in Indianapolis, IN.

Jamie loves to spend time with his beautiful wife and two daughters (and dog and two cats), and has a great time playing drums at an awesome local church. Jamie also continually seeks opportunities to share his passion for helping software teams rapidly deliver real and measurable value to their customers.

About the Technical Reviewer

Jeff Sanders is a published author, technical editor, and accomplished technologist. He is currently employed with Symbolic Systems as a Portfolio Delivery Manager and Senior Solutions Architect.

Jeff has years of professional experience in the field of IT and strategic business consulting leading both sales and delivery efforts. He regularly contributes to certification and product roadmap development with Microsoft, and he speaks publicly on Microsoft enterprise technologies. With his roots in software development, Jeff's areas of expertise include collaboration and content-management solutions, operational intelligence, digital marketing, distributed component-based application architectures, object-oriented analysis and design, and enterprise integration patterns and designs.

Jeff is also the CTO of DynamicShift, a client-focused organization specializing in Microsoft technologies, including Office365/BPOS, SharePoint Server, StreamInsight, Windows Azure, AppFabric, Business Activity Monitoring, BizTalk Server, and .NET. He is a Microsoft Certified Trainer, and leads DynamicShift in both training and consulting efforts.

He enjoys non-work-related travel, spending time with his wife and daughter, and wishes he had more time for both

He may be reached at jeff.sanders@dynamicshift.com.

Acknowledgments

I would like to thank everyone at Apress for listening to me and giving me the opportunity to share my love for success in technology with others in the .NET community. In particular, I want to thank Ewan Buckingham for getting this book off the ground and holding my hand as it developed from concept into something readable. I also want to thank Jill Balzano, who worked tirelessly with me and many others to make sure all of the pieces came together according to the usual Apress excellence.

Thank you, as well, to the technical reviewer, Jeff Sanders, who not only provided great technical feedback, but also brought many years of authorship experience to the table, helping me to craft the overall message of the book.

Finally, I want to thank a few people from my personal life, all of whom have played key roles in getting me here. My mom, Lynn Crandall, a writer herself, has provided encouragement and practical guidance when I really had no idea where to start. My friend and coworker, Brian Wortman, has shown never-ending patience for my sometimes annoying drive and extreme bluntness. I greatly appreciate his steadfast determination to teach me better ways of doing things, which has made this book a possibility. Most of the really good stuff in this book came from him, borne out of some heated argument, lunchtime discussion, or long debate over email. Brian also happily tech reviewed every inch of this book—without even getting paid! Thanks also to a recent boss and new friend, Jeff Pickett who shares my vision and hunger for building a career and personal brand that is more than just going to work every day. He has provided just the right amount of nudging and brainstorming needed at just the right time. Here's to many more dreams over coffee, Jeff.

Thank you all so much.
Jamie Kurtz

CHAPTER 1

■ ■ ■

ASP.NET MVC as a Service Framework

In the years since the first release of the .NET Framework, Microsoft has provided a variety of approaches for building service-oriented applications. Starting back in 2002 with the original release of .NET, a developer could fairly easily create an ASP.NET ASMX-based XML web service that allowed other .NET and non-.NET clients to call it. Those web services implemented various versions of SOAP, but were only available for use over HTTP.

In addition to web services, the 1.0 release of .NET provided support for Remoting. This allowed developers to write services that weren't necessarily tied to the HTTP protocol. Similar to ASMX-based web services, .NET Remoting essentially provides object activation and session context for client-initiated method calls. The caller uses a proxy object to invoke methods, and the .NET runtime handles serialization and marshaling of data between the client's proxy object and the server's activated service object.

Towards the end of 2006, Microsoft released .NET 3.0, which included the Windows Communication Foundation (WCF). WCF not only replaced ASMX web services and .NET Remoting, but also took a giant step forward in the way of flexibility, configurability, extensibility, and support for more recent security and other SOAP standards. For example, with WCF, a developer can write a non-HTTP service that supports authentication with SAML tokens, and host it in a custom-built Windows service. These and other capabilities greatly broaden the scenarios under which .NET can be utilized to build a service-oriented application.

MORE ON WCF

If you're interested in learning more about WCF, I recommend reading either *Programming WCF Services* by Juval Lowy [O'Reilly, 2007] or *Essential Windows Communication Foundation* by Steve Resnick, Richard Crane, and Chris Bowen [Addison-Wesley Professional, 2008]. Both of these books are appropriate for WCF novices and veterans alike, as they cover the spectrum from basic to advanced WCF topics.

If you need to set up communication between two applications, whether they are co-located or separated by thousands of miles, rest-assured WCF can do it. And if its out-of-the-box features don't suffice, WCF's tremendous extensibility model provides ample opportunity for plugging in just about anything you can think of.

And this is where we will take a bit of a left turn, off the evolutionary path of ever greater capability and flexibility, and towards something simpler and more targeted at a small set of specific scenarios.

In the Land of JavaScript and Mobile Devices

During much of the growth of the Internet over the past two-plus decades, web sites and pages have relied on server-side code for anything but basic HTML manipulation. But more recently, various AJAX-related tools and frameworks—including (but not limited to) JavaScript, jQuery, HTML5, and some tricks with CSS—have given rise to the need for services that are less about complex enterprise applications talking to each other and more about web pages needing to get and push small amounts of data. In these cases, communicating with a service over HTTP is pretty much a given, since the web sites themselves are HTTP applications. Further, security options available from within a browser are vastly simpler than those of an out-of-browser application, and thus support for all of the various security-related SOAP standards is not required of the service.

In addition to simpler protocol and security needs, web pages typically communicate with other applications and services using text-based messages rather than binary-formatted messages. As such, a service needs only to support XML or JSON serialization.

Beyond web applications, today's smartphones and tablets have created a huge demand for services in support of small smart-client mobile applications. These services are very similar in nature to those that support AJAX-enabled web sites. For example, they typically communicate via HTTP; they send and receive small amounts of text-based data; and their security models tend to take a minimalist approach in order to provide a better user experience (i.e., they strive for less configuration and fewer headaches for users). Also, the implementation of these services encourages more reuse across the different mobile platforms.

In short, there is now a desire for a service framework that, out-of-the-box, provides exactly what is needed for these simple text-based HTTP services. While WCF can be used to create such services, it is definitely not configured that way by default. Unfortunately, the added flexibility and configurability of WCF make it all too easy to mess something up.

And this is where the ASP.NET MVC Framework comes into the picture.

Advantages of Using the MVC Framework

Once you know that, under certain scenarios, you aren't interested in many of the capabilities of WCF, you can start thinking of a framework like ASP.NET MVC—with fewer service-oriented bells and whistles—as being advantageous. In this section, you'll look in detail at a few of these.

Configuration

As is the case when building a web site, there isn't much to configure to get an MVC-based service up and running. The concept of endpoints doesn't exist, and neither do contracts. As you'll see later, an MVC-based service is pretty loose in comparison to a WCF service. You pretty much just need a REST URL, a set of inbound arguments, and a response JSON or XML message.

REST by Default

Speaking of REST, building services with ASP.NET MVC and the Web API provides most of what you need to adhere to the constraints of the REST architecture. This is largely due to the URL routing feature provided by the MVC Framework. Unlike WCF, where a service is an address to a physical file (i.e., an address that maps directly to a service class or .svc file), service addresses with MVC are REST–style routes that map to controller methods. As such, the paths lend themselves very nicely to REST–style API specifications.

This concept of routing is critical to understanding how MVC can be used for building services, so let's look at an example. In this book you will learn how to develop a simple task-management service. You can imagine having a service method to fetch a single task. This method would take a task's TaskId and return that task. Implemented in WCF, the method might look like this:

```
[ServiceContract]
public interface ITaskService
{
    [OperationContract]
    Task GetTask(long taskId);
}

public class TaskService : ITaskService
{
    private readonly IRepository _repository;

    public TaskService(IRepository repository)
    {
        _repository = repository;
    }

    public Task GetTask(long taskId)
    {
        return _repository.Get<Task>(taskId);
    }
}
```

With an appropriately configured .svc file and corresponding endpoint, you would have a URL that looks similar to this:

```
http://MyServer/TaskService.svc
```

The caller would then post a SOAP request with the SOAP action set to GetTask, passing in the TaskId argument. Of course, when building a .NET client, much of the underlying SOAP gunk is taken care of for you. But making SOAP calls from JavaScript can a bit more challenging, and—arguably—unnecessary.

This same example under ASP.NET MVC4 would involve creating a controller instead of a WCF service class. The method for fetching a Task object exists on the controller, but it is no longer defined by a contract, as it is in WCF. The controller might look like this:

```
public class TasksController : Controller
{
    private readonly IRepository _repository;

    public TasksController(IRepository repository)
    {
        _repository = repository;
    }

    public ActionResult Get(long taskId)
    {
        return Json(_repository.Get<Task>(taskId));
    }
}
```

With the TasksController, and an appropriately configured route, the URL used to fetch a single task would like this:

```
http://MyServer/Task/Get/123
```

Note that the method name "Get" appears in the URL. Let's look briefly at an example built with the Web API:

```
public class TasksController : ApiController
{
    private readonly IRepository _repository;

    public TasksController(IRepository repository)
    {
        _repository = repository;
    }
```

```
public Task Get(long taskId)
{
    return repository.Get<Task>(taskId);
}
}
```

One of the biggest changes is the base class used by the new controller, ApiController. This base class was built specifically for enabling RESTful services, and you simply return the object (or, objects in a collection) of the data being requested. Contrast this with the ActionResult shown in the preceding MVC4 example. Further, the URL itself will be different:

```
http://MyServer/Tasks/123
```

Note how the URL no longer needs to include the controller's method name. This is because, with the Web API, HTTP verbs (e.g. GET, POST, PUT) are automatically mapped to corresponding controller methods. As you'll see in the next chapter, this helps you create an API that adheres more closely with the tenets of the REST architecture.

For now, the important thing to realize is that the entirety of this service call is contained in the URL itself; there is no SOAP message to go along with the address. And this is one of the key tenets of REST: resources are accessible via unique URIs.

A QUICK OVERVIEW OF REST

Created by Roy Fielding, one of the primary authors of the HTTP specification, REST is meant to take better advantage of standards and technologies within HTTP than SOAP does today. For example, rather than creating arbitrary SOAP methods, developers of REST APIs are encouraged to use only HTTP verbs:

- GET

- POST

- PUT

- DELETE

REST is also resource-centric; that is, RESTful APIs use HTTP verbs to act on or fetch information about resources. These would be the nouns in REST parlance (e.g., Tasks, Users, Customers, and Orders). Thus, you have verbs acting on nouns. Another way of saying this is that you perform actions against a resource.

Additionally, REST takes advantage of other aspects of HTTP systems, such as the following:

- Caching

- Security

- Statelessness

- Network layering (with various firewalls and gateways in between client and server)

This book will cover REST principles sufficiently for you to build services using ASP.NET MVC. However, if you're interested, you can find several good books that cover the full breadth of the REST architecture. You might also find it interesting to read Chapter 5 of Fielding's doctoral dissertation, where the idea of REST was first conceived. You can find that chapter here:

`http://www.ics.uci.edu/~fielding/pubs/dissertation/rest_arch_style.htm`

Before moving on, let's address a point that some may be thinking about: you can indeed create REST services with WCF. Looking around the Internet, you can certainly find arguments on both sides of the MVC versus WCF debate (for building RESTful services). Since this is a book on how to build services with MVC and the Web API, let's skip that debate altogether.

Abstraction with Routes

Somewhat similar to service interfaces and their implementations in WCF, routes give the MVC service developer a layer of abstraction between what the callers see and the underlying implementation. In other words, you can map any URL to any controller method. When the API signature (i.e., the REST URL) isn't hard-wired to a particular interface, class, or .svc file, you are free to update your implementation of that API method, as long as the URL specification for that method remains valid.

One classic example of using URLs to handle changing implementations is in the case of service versioning. By creating a new route with a "v2" (or similar) embedded in the URL, you can create an arbitrary mapping between an implementation and a versioning scheme or set of versions that doesn't exist until sometime later. Thus, you can take a set of controllers (and their methods) and decide a year from now that they will be part of the v2 API.

Controller Activation Is, Well, Very Nice

Whether the subject is the older XML Web Services (a.k.a. ASMX services), WCF, or services with ASP.NET MVC, the concept of *service activation* is present. Essentially, since by-and-large all calls to a service are new requests, the ASP.NET or WCF runtime activates a new instance of the service class for each request. This is similar to object instantiation in OO-speak. Note that service activation is a little more involved than simply having the application code create a new object; this book will touch on this topic in more depth in later chapters.

ASP.NET MVC provides a simple mechanism for pre- and post-processing called *action filters*. These filters are essentially classes that contain a few methods allowing you to run some code before and after the controller methods are invoked. These action filters take the form of attributes, and they are either decorated on specific methods or configured globally for all methods.

It's a bit tough to describe, but once you write and debug a few controllers—along with some action filters—you will start noticing how clean and easy Microsoft has made this arrangement. Nothing is hidden from you, making it simple to understand and step through an entire service call in the debugger.

Interoperability of JSON, XML, and REST

As mentioned previously, REST is based solely on existing HTTP standards, so it is extremely interoperable across all platforms capable of making HTTP requests. This not only includes computers, smartphones, and tablets, but it also gets into devices such as normal "old-fashioned" cell phones, DVRs, phone systems, ATM machines, refrigerators, alarm systems, browsers, digital watches—and the list goes on. As long as the device can make an HTTP request to a URL, it can "do" REST.

The same applies to JSON and straight XML data. Compared to SOAP, these technologies require very little in the way of proper formatting or an understanding of message specifications. Technically speaking, SOAP is an XML-based protocol. However, constructing a valid SOAP message (including envelope, header, and body) is quite a bit more complex than simply representing just your data with XML. The same can be said of parsing XML or JSON versus full-blown SOAP messages. And this complexity means that developers typically need SOAP libraries in order to construct and parse SOAP messages. The need for these libraries limits SOAP's usability on small or specialty devices.

One of the main advantages of JSON, other than its drop-dead simplistic formatting, is that, for a given data package, it is much smaller in size than the same data represented as XML/SOAP. Again, this makes JSON very appealing for occasionally-connected or low-power devices, as well as those that are most often used over cellular networks.

This is not to say SOAP isn't valuable or doesn't have its place; quite the contrary, actually. The capabilities of the SOAP protocol go far beyond those of REST and JSON. Most of these capabilities are defined by the WS-* specifications ("WS" stands for "web services"). These specifications deal with more complex messaging needs such as message security, transactions, service discovery, metadata publishing, routing, trust relationships, and identity federation. None of these are possible with REST, as they require capabilities outside the scope of the HTTP protocol.

A Brief Introduction to the Web API

None of the aspects and advantages of using ASP.NET MVC discussed so far have had anything to do with the new MVC4 Web API. In truth, the MVC Framework itself—without the Web API—provides a simple yet powerful framework for building REST-based services.

That said, the new Web API available in MVC4 kicks things up yet another notch. It brings a whole slew of features that make it even easier and faster to build REST services. Let's look at just a few of these new features:

- **Convention-based CRUD Actions:** HTTP actions (e.g., GET and POST) are automatically mapped to controller methods (also known as *controller actions*) by their names. For example, on a controller called Products, a GET request such as /api/products will automatically invoke a method named "Get" on the controller. Further, the Web API automatically matches the number of arguments given in the URL to an appropriate controller method. Therefore, the URL /api/products/32 would automatically invoke the Get(long id) method. The same magic also applies to POST, PUT, and DELETE calls.

- **Built-in Content Negotiation:** In MVC, controller methods that return JSON or XML have to be hard-coded to specifically return one of those content types. But with the Web API, the controller method need only return the raw data value, and this value will be automatically converted to JSON or XML, per the caller's request. The caller simply uses an Accept or Content-Type HTTP header to specify the desired content type of the returned data, and the Web API ensures your return value gets formatted appropriately. Rather than returning an object of type JsonResult, you simply return your data object (e.g., Product or IEnumerable<Product>).

- **Automatic support for OData:** By simply placing the new [Queryable] attribute on a controller method that returns IQueryable, clients can use the method for OData query composition.

- **Self-hosting:** With the Web API, you no longer need to use IIS to host HTTP services. Now your REST services can be hosted in a custom Windows service, console application, or any other type of host you need.

Summary

In this chapter, you learned how the ASP.NET MVC Framework provides a great platform for building REST-style Web APIs. In scenarios where much of the power and flexibility of WCF and SOAP aren't needed, MVC can be a very simple and elegant alternative. These scenarios include applications that need to support only HTTP communication, as well as those that focus heavily on text-formatted messages.

You also learned about the various advantages of using ASP.NET MVC, including great support for REST, custom URL routes, and the interoperability of REST- and JSON-based services.

Finally, you were introduced to the all-new Web API and explored a few of the features it brings to the world of ASP.NET-based REST services.

CHAPTER 2

■ ■ ■

What is RESTful?

This chapter explores what a service following the REST architecture should look like. Considering that such an API is, in theory, supposed to use the HTTP verbs and be focused on resources, its interface will be markedly different from your typical RPC-style API. So, as we design the service, we will compare the REST approach with a more traditional RPC or SOAP approach.

Throughout this book, we will be working on a service for managing tasks. It's not terribly exciting, I know; however, the lack of domain excitement will let you focus on the technical aspects of the service. Designing a RESTful interface is trickier than you might think, and you will need to reprogram your brain to some degree to go about modeling such an API.

The fact that this is more work up front certainly doesn't mean you shouldn't follow this path. As briefly covered in the previous chapter, there are many benefits to the REST architecture. But it will take some work to realize those benefits. Creating a REST API is not as simple as just converting your RPC methods into REST URLs, as many like to imagine. You must work within the constraints of the architecture. And, in this case, you must also work within the constraints of the HTTP protocol because that will be your platform.

Here's what you'll learn about in this chapter:

- Leonard Richardson's maturity model for REST

- Working with URIs and resources

- Working with HTTP verbs

- Returning appropriate HTTP status codes

Let's get started.

From RPC to REST

In November 2008, a fellow by the name of Leonard Richardson created a maturity model for REST. A maturity model, by definition, is a map that guides the user into ever-increasing levels of compliance with a given definition, architecture, or methodology. For example, the model called Capability Maturity Model Integration (CMMI) was created as a process-improvement approach to help organizations (typically, software organizations) improve performance and increase efficiencies. The model contains five *levels*, where each successive level is designed to provide the user or organization more process efficiency over the previous level.

Richardson's REST Maturity Model (RMM) provides service API developers the same type of improvement map for building RESTful web services. His model, in fact, starts at level 0 with a RPC-style interface, and then progresses up through three more levels—at which point you've achieved an API interface design that is, at least, according to Roy Fielding,[1] a pre-condition for a RESTful service. That is, you cannot claim to have a RESTful service if you stop at levels 0, 1, or 2 of the RMM; however, it's certainly possible to screw things up to the extent that you don't have a RESTful service at level 3, either.

Figure 2-1 summarizes the levels in the RMM.

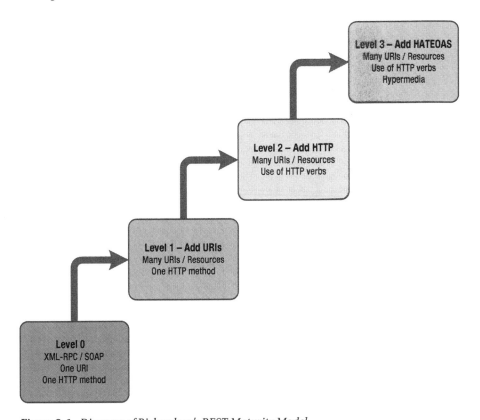

Figure 2-1. *Diagram of Richardson's REST Maturity Model*

---

[1] http://roy.gbiv.com/untangled/2008/rest-apis-must-be-hypertext-driven

XML-RPC and SOAP

At Level 0, the API resembles most SOAP services. That is, the interface is characterized by having a single URI that supports only a single HTTP method or verb. You'll learn more about the available verbs in a bit; but for now, just know that HTTP provides a small set of known verbs that must be used if you intend to conform to and capitalize on the protocol.

Suppose, as mentioned in Chapter 1, that you want to build a task-management service, and you need to provide a way to create new tasks through a new API. If this were a Level 0 SOAP-based service, you might create a WCF service class called TaskService; and on it you might create a new method called CreateTask(). This method might take a request message that includes a task title, task category, perhaps a status, and so on. And the method's response message would likely include, among other things, a system-generated task number.

You also might create a method for fetching the details of a task. So, on your TaskService class, you might add a method called GetTask(). This new method would likely take as input a task ID of some kind, and then return a task object—serialized as XML.

To round out the TaskService class, you might also add the methods UpdateTask(), SearchTasks(), and CompleteTask(). Each of these would be designed to take in appropriate XML request messages and return some kind of response message.

The REST Maturity Model—and indeed the work published by Roy Fielding—provides three distinct web-related attributes of an API that help you position yourself to be RESTful with HTTP:

- Unique URIs to resources

- Consistent use of HTTP verbs

- "Hypermedia as the engine of application state" (HATEOAS)

Let's examine the pretend TaskService service interface using these three attributes (see Table 2-1).

Table 2-1. *Task Service at Level 0 on the RMM*

Method	URI	HTTP verb	State changes/contract
CreateTask	/api/taskService.svc	POST	Caller required to know (e.g., WSDL)
GetTask	/api/taskService.svc	POST	Caller required to know (e.g., WSDL)
GetTaskAssignees	/api/taskService.svc	POST	Caller required to know (e.g., WSDL)
SearchTasks	/api/taskService.svc	POST	Caller required to know (e.g., WSDL)
UpdateTask	/api/taskService.svc	POST	Caller required to know (e.g., WSDL)
CompleteTask	/api/taskService.svc	POST	Caller required to know (e.g., WSDL)

As you can see, each operation or method on the service looks the same—when looked at from the point of view of the Web. And the service doesn't look and feel very Web-like. For example, whether fetching task 123 or task 456, the URI is the same. In fact, it is also the same URI used to create a task, update a task, complete a task, and so on. There's no sense of resource or resource addressability in our URI—that is, there's no URI that points directly to a specific task or list of tasks.

This example also does not utilize HTTP verbs as intended. This was discussed a bit in Chapter 1, and you'll learn about this in more detail later; however, every action available in the API is essentially custom-made. To be RESTful on HTTP, you need to avoid creating custom actions and instead support actions that are consistent with HTTP. In other words, you need to use GET, PUT, POST, and DELETE (to name the primary actions).

And finally, clients are required to know all of the available actions ahead of time. This means there is an implicit binding between client and server, in that the caller is dependent on a contract and a given set of actions from the service. Again, this does not feel very Web-like. When you browse to a public website, all you are required to remember is the root address. From there, everything else is discoverable and linked to other elements via hypermedia (i.e., links and forms). Indeed, hypermedia is the engine of application state. You can transition from one state to the next (where the state machine is a web site or the broader Internet) based solely on links and forms. You are not required to remember or know ahead of time the specific addresses for all of the pages you intend to traverse.

You are also not required to remember every field that must be filled out on a form when submitting a request (e.g., placing an order or signing up for a magazine subscription). Essentially, the server dictates all of the relationships, all of the URIs, and all of the forms—without you needing any prior knowledge. So, if any of these properties change, you likely wouldn't even notice or care. This is because we, the clients, have an implicit understanding with web sites: they will guide us through available resources and provide all the information we need in order to make any changes or requests.

As you'll see shortly, this attribute of HATEOAS is key to a service's RESTfulness; however, it is often overlooked as it requires a significant shift in thinking from the traditional RPC-style interface design.

URIs and Resources

As noted briefly in Chapter 1, building a RESTful interface means you end up with an API that is very resource-centric. As such, you need to intentionally design the interface with resources being at the center. Unlike RPC-style interfaces, where arbitrary service methods (i.e., the verbs) and their associated request and response messages rule the day, a REST interface will revolve around the resources (i.e., the nouns). The actions available to those resources are constrained by the use of HTTP. This is why you must map the available HTTP verbs into the API; you don't have the freedom to create other actions or verbs.

This concept is central to a REST design. So let's examine what the TaskService might look like if it were to be a level 1 on the RMM. Table 2-2 shows how each individual resource is addressable by a unique URI.

Table 2-2. *Task Service at Level 1 on the RMM*

Method	URI	HTTP verb	State changes/contract
CreateTask	/api/tasks	POST	Caller required to know (e.g., WSDL)
GetTask	/api/tasks/1234	POST	Caller required to know (e.g., WSDL)
GetTaskAssignees	/api/tasks/1234	POST	Caller required to know (e.g., WSDL)
SearchTasks	/api/tasks	POST	Caller required to know (e.g., WSDL)
UpdateTask	/api/tasks/1234	POST	Caller required to know (e.g., WSDL)
CompleteTask	/api/tasks/1234	POST	Caller required to know (e.g., WSDL)

But you still must rely on specific messages for operations. In other words, the caller can't differentiate between the two different operations available with the /api/tasks URI—unless the caller already has the contract. You're still using only the POST HTTP verb, so the request message itself dictates the desired action.

HTTP Verbs

You must look beyond URIs and their resources to the actions needed by the service. These actions will help you identify the HTTP verbs you need to use. Continuing to follow our example, there's no such thing as a CreateTask HTTP verb. In fact, there's not even a Create verb. If you're going to follow the REST architecture and the HTTP protocol, you must choose from the verbs available in that protocol, namely:

- GET
- PUT
- POST
- DELETE

Intuitively, you can quickly eliminate GET and DELETE for the CreateTask action. But what is the difference in intent between PUT and POST? As shown in Table 2-3, PUT is designed to create or replace a resource with a known identifier—and hence a known unique URI. You use a POST when the system is generating the new resource's identifier.

Table 2-3. *Using HTTP verbs with the Task Resource*

HTTP verb	(Collection URI) `http://myserver.com/tasks`	(Element URI) `http://myserver.com/tasks/1234`
GET	List of tasks, including URIs to individual tasks	Get a specific task, identified by the URI
PUT	Replace the entire collection of tasks	Replace or create the single task identified by the URI
POST	Create a new single task, where its identifier is generated by the system	Create a new subordinate under the task identified by the URI
DELETE	Delete the entire collection of tasks	Delete the tasks identified by the URI

Technically speaking, the REST architecture is agnostic about any specific protocol. That includes the HTTP protocol. In other words, all you need is a protocol that provides a language and mechanism for describing both states (i.e., *representations*) and state changes. However, since this book is about building a REST service with ASP.NET, you'll focus on REST with HTTP. Fortunately, the HTTP protocol itself covers most of what you need. Again, Table 2-3 illustrates the intended use of the verbs within REST.

Let's walk through some important concepts with this mapping. First, the exact meaning of each of the four verbs is dependent on the URI. So even though you have only four verbs, you actually have eight different actions available to you. The difference lies in whether the URI defines a collection or a unique element.

Second, when creating new instances of the resource (e.g. a new task), PUT is used with a unique URI in the scenario where the caller generates the new resource's identifier before submitting the request to the server. In Table 2-3, the PUT action is used with a unique element URI to create a new task with the specific identifier, 1234. If instead the system is to generate the identifier, then the caller uses the POST action and a collection URI. This also ties into the concept of *idempotency.*

The PUT and DELETE methods are said to be idempotent; that is, calling them over and over will produce the same result without any additional side effects. For example, the caller should be able to call the DELETE action on a specific resource without receiving any errors and without harming the system. If the resource has already been deleted, the caller should not receive an error. The same applies to the PUT action. For a given unique resource (identified by an element URI), submitting a PUT request should update the resource if it already exists. Or, if it doesn't exist, the system should create the resource as submitted. In other words, calling PUT over and over produces the same result without any additional side effects (i.e., the new task will exist in the system per the representation provided by the caller, whether the system had to create a new one or it had to update an existing one).

The GET action is said to be *safe.* This is not idempotent, per se. Safe means that nothing in the system is changed at all, which is appropriate for HTTP calls that are meant to query the system for either a collection of resources or for a specific resource.

It is important that the idempotency of the service's GET, PUT, and DELETE operations remain consistent with the HTTP protocol standards. Thus, every effort should be made to ensure those three actions can be called over and over without error.

Unlike the other three actions, POST is not considered to be idempotent. This is because POST is used to create a new instance of the identified resource type for every invocation of the method. Where calling PUT over and over will never result in more than one resource being created or updated, calling POST will result in new resource instances—one for each call. This is appropriate for cases where the system must generate the new resource's identifier, as well as return it in the response.

As you model your task-management service, you will need to map each resource with a set of HTTP actions, defining which ones are allowed and which ones aren't supported.

Now let's take a new look at the task service. This time around, you'll use the available HTTP verbs, which will put you at level 2 on the RMM (see Table 2-4).

Table 2-4. *Task Service at Level 2 in the RMM*

Method	URI	HTTP verb	State changes/contract
CreateTask	/api/tasks	POST	Caller required to know (e.g., WSDL)
GetTask	/api/tasks/1234	GET	Caller required to know (e.g., WSDL)
GetTaskAssignees	/api/tasks/1234/users	GET	Caller required to know (e.g., WSDL)
SearchTasks	/api/tasks	GET	Caller required to know (e.g., WSDL)
UpdateTask	/api/tasks/1234	PUT	Caller required to know (e.g., WSDL)
CompleteTask	/api/tasks/1234	DELETE	Caller required to know (e.g., WSDL)

At this point, the service is utilizing unique URIs for individual resources, and you've switched to using HTTP verbs instead of custom request message types. That is, each of the PUT and POST actions mentioned previously will simply take a representation of a task resource (e.g., XML or JSON). However, the client must still have prior knowledge of the API in order to traverse the domain and to perform any operations more complex than creating, updating, or completing a task. In the true nature of the Web, you should instead fully guide the client, providing all available resources and actions via links and forms. This is what is meant by "hypermedia as the engine of application state."

HATEOAS

As you look at Tables 2-3 and 2-4, you can see that certain GET operations will return collections of resources. One of the guiding principles of REST with HTTP is that callers make transitions through application state only by navigating hypermedia provided by the server. In other words, given a root or starting URI, the caller should be able to navigate the collection of resources without needing prior knowledge of the URI scheme. Thus, whenever a resource is returned from the service, whether in a collection or by itself, the returned data should include the URI required to turn around and perform another GET to retrieve just that resource.

Here's an example of an XML response message that illustrates how each element in the collection should contain a URI to the resource:

```xml
<?xml version="1.0" encoding="utf-8"?>
<Tasks>
    <Task Id="1234" Status="Active" >
        <link rel="self" href="/api/tasks/1234" method="GET" />
    </Task>
    <Task Id="0987" Status="Completed" >
        <link rel="self" href="/api/tasks/0987" method="GET" />
    </Task>
</Tasks>
```

It is typically appropriate to return only a few attributes or pieces of data when responding with a collection, such as in the preceding example. Now the caller can use the URI to query a specific resource to retrieve all attributes of that resource. For example, the Tasks collection response (as just shown) might only contain the Task's Id and a URI to fetch the Task resource. But when calling GET to get a specific Task, the response might include TaskCategory, DateCreated, TaskStatus, TaskOwner, and so on.

Taking this approach can be a little trickier when using strongly typed model objects in .NET (or any other OO language). This is because we need to define at least two different variants of the Task type. The typical pattern is to have a TaskInfo class and a Task class, where the TaskInfo class exists only to provide basic information about a Task. The collection might look like this:

```xml
<?xml version="1.0" encoding="utf-8"?>
<Tasks>
    <TaskInfo Id="1234" Status="Active" >
        <link rel="self" href="/api/tasks/1234" method="GET" />
    </TaskInfo>
    <TaskInfo Id="0987" Status="Completed" >
        <link rel="self" href="/api/tasks/0987" method="GET" />
    </TaskInfo>
</Tasks>
```

And the single resource might look like this:

```xml
<?xml version="1.0" encoding="utf-8"?>
<Task Id="1234" Status="Active" DateCreated="2011-08-15" Owner="Sally"
Category="Projects" >
    <link rel="self" href="/api/tasks/1234" method="GET" />
</Task>
```

Utilizing two different types like this is not a requirement for REST or any other service API-style. You may find that you don't need to separate collection type definitions from other definitions. Or, you may find that you need many more than two. It all depends on the usage scenarios and how many different attributes exist on the resource. For example, if the Task resource included only five or six attributes, then you probably wouldn't create a separate type for the collection objects. But if the Task object were to include 100 or more attributes (as is typical in any real-life financial application), then it might be a good idea to create more than one variation of the Task type.

Within the realm of HATEOAS, you also want to guide the user as to the actions available on a resource. You just saw how you can use a <link> element to provide a reference for fetching task details. You can expand this concept to include all available resources and actions. Remember, when browsing a web site, a user needs to have prior knowledge only of the root address to traverse the entire site. You want to provide a similar experience to callers in the API.

Here's what a full HATEOAS-compliant XML response might look like for the TaskInfo type:

```xml
<?xml version="1.0" encoding="utf-8"?>
<Tasks>
    <TaskInfo Id="1234" Status="Active" >
        <link rel="self" href="/api/tasks/1234" method="GET" />
        <link rel="users" href="/api/tasks/1234/users" method="GET" />
        <link rel="history" href="/api/tasks/1234/history" method="GET" />
        <link rel="complete" href="/api/tasks/1234" method="DELETE" />
        <link rel="update" href="/api/tasks/1234" method="PUT" />
    </TaskInfo>
    <TaskInfo Id="0987" Status="Completed" >
        <link rel="self" href="/api/tasks/0987" method="GET" />
        <link rel="users" href="/api/tasks/0987/users" method="GET" />
        <link rel="history" href="/api/tasks/0987/history" method="GET" />
        <link rel="reopen" href="/api/tasks/0987" method="PUT" />
    </TaskInfo>
</Tasks>
```

Note that the links available to each task are a little different. This is because you don't need to complete an already completed task. Instead, you need to offer a link to reopen it. Also, you don't want to allow updates on a completed task, so that link is not present in the completed task.

LINK PHILOSOPHY

I want to offer a disclaimer and a word of warning for the topic of links in REST messages. You find that, over the past several years, the debate over how the HTTP verbs are supposed to be used can be quite heated at times. This debate also extends into how to best design URIs to be most RESTful—without degenerating into SOAP-style API.

For example, in the Task XML you just looked at, it specifies the "reopen" link as a PUT to the /api/tasks/0987 URI. It also specifies the "complete" link as a DELETE to the /api/tasks/1234 URI. These approaches are neither specified by the REST architecture, nor are they even agreed upon by the folks that practice REST. And for whatever reason, people on various sides of the debate tend to get worked up about their way of doing things.

Instead of using a PUT against the resource URI for the "reopen" action, you could instead use a PUT against a URI like /api/tasks/0987/reopen. I tend to lean away from this approach, as it pushes you closer to specifying actions instead of resources (for the URI). However, I also think it's a bit unrealistic to assume you can accommodate all available actions on something like a Task object with only four HTTP verbs. Indeed, there are a few more verbs you can use, including PATCH, HEAD, and OPTIONS. But even so, the set of available verbs is limited, and the REST architecture dictates that you don't add to those verbs. So at some point, you need to make a judgment call as to how to implement various actions on the Task object. The important thing is to conform as closely to HTTP standards as possible.

The use of the DELETE verb is also hotly debated. Most enterprise applications don't allow the caller to really delete a resource. More often, a resource is merely closed, inactivated, hidden, and so on. As such, it might seem reasonable to not waste one of your precious few verbs on an action that you never even allow, when instead you could use it for the "close" action.

As with most endeavors in the world of software, the devil's in the details. And you can usually find 101 ways to implement those details if you look hard enough. My advice here is to simply do the best you can, don't be afraid to be wrong, and don't get stuck in an infinite loop of forever debating the very best approach to follow. Think, commit, and go.

You can now complete the table of task resources and operations using the three concepts you've learned from the RMM:

- URIs and resources

- HTTP verbs

- HATEOAS

Table 2-5 illustrates the task service under a more ideal RESTful design. That is, it shows the things you can do to make the service self-describing (i.e., related information and available operations are given to the caller via links contained in the service's responses). Again, following the RMM isn't sufficient in itself to being able to claim your service is a REST service. That said, you can't claim compliance with REST without following it, either.

Table 2-5. *Task Service at Level 3 in the RMM*

Method	URI	HTTP verb	State changes/contract
CreateTask	/api/tasks	POST	HTTP POST used for creation
GetTask	/api/tasks/1234	GET	HTTP GET always fetches
GetTaskAssignees	/api/tasks/1234/users	GET	GET on users is self-describing
SearchTasks	/api/tasks	GET	Get on tasks is self-describing
UpdateTask	/api/tasks/1234	PUT	HTTP PUT on a task updates
CompleteTask	/api/tasks/1234	DELETE	HTTP DELETE on a task deletes or inactivates

There is one last bit of guidance to discuss before wrapping up this exploration of REST.

HTTP Status Codes

So far in this chapter, you've learned about the constraints of the REST architecture that led to creating an API where resources are the message of choice; where every resource and every action on a resource has a unique URI; where, instead of creating custom methods or actions, you're limiting yourself to the actions available with HTTP; and, finally, where you're giving the caller every action available on a given resource. All of these constraints deal with calls made by the caller. The last thing to discuss deals with the messages you send back from the server in response to those calls.

In the same way that you are constrained to using only the verbs available with HTTP, you are also constrained to using only the well-known set of HTTP status codes as return "codes" for your service calls. That is not to say you can't include additional information, of course. In fact, every web page you visit includes an HTTP status code, in addition to the HTML you see in the browser. The basic idea here is simply to utilize known status codes in the response headers.

Let's look first at a subset of the available HTTP status codes. You can find the complete official specification here: www.w3.org/Protocols/rfc2616/rfc2616-sec10.html. In this section, you will only be examining a small subset of these codes. Table 2-6 lists the most common status codes and their descriptions in the context of a RESTful API.

Table 2-6. *A List of Common HTTP Status Codes*

Status Code	API meaning
200	All is good; response will include applicable resource information, as well
201	Resource created; will include the Location header specifying a URI to the newly created resource
202	Same as 200, but used for async; in other words, all is good, but we need to poll the service to find out when completed
301	The resource was moved; should include URI to new location
400	Bad request; caller should reformat the request
401	Unauthorized; should respond with an authentication challenge, to let the caller resubmit with appropriate credentials
403	Access denied; user successfully authenticated, but is not allowed to access the requested resource
404	Resource not found, or, caller not allowed to access the resource and we don't want to reveal the reason
409	Conflict; used as a response to a PUT request when another caller has dirtied the resource
500	Server error; something bad happened, and server might include some indication of the underlying problem

For example, assume a caller submitted the following HTTP request:

```
GET /api/tasks/1234 HTTP/1.1
```

The service should respond as follows (this is the raw HTTP response):

```
HTTP/1.1 200 OK
Content-Type: application/xml

<Task Id="1234" Status="Active" DateCreated="2011-08-15" Owner="Sally"
Category="Projects" >
    <link rel="self" href="/api/tasks/1234" method="GET" />
    <link rel="users" href="/api/tasks/1234/users" method="GET" />
    <link rel="complete" href="/api/tasks/1234" method="DELETE" />
    <link rel="update" href="/api/tasks/1234" method="PUT" />
</Task>
```

Suppose now the caller is using a POST request to create a new task:

```
POST /api/tasks HTTP/1.1
Content-Type: application/xml

<Task Status="Active" DateCreated="2012-08-15" Owner="Jimmy"
Category="Projects" >
```

The service should respond with a 201 code and the new task's URI (assuming the call succeeded):

```
HTTP/1.1 201 Created
Location: /api/tasks/6789
Content-Type: application/xml

<Task Id="6789" Status="Active" DateCreated="2012-08-15" Owner="Jimmy"
Category="Projects" >
    <link rel="self" href="/api/tasks/6789" method="GET" />
    <link rel="owner" href="/api/tasks/6789/owner" method="GET" />
    <link rel="complete" href="/api/tasks/6789" method="DELETE" />
    <link rel="update" href="/api/tasks/6789" method="PUT" />
</Task>
```

The main point here, which is consistent with the topics discussed throughout this chapter, is to utilize the HTTP protocol as much as you can. That is really the crux of REST with HTTP: you both use HTTP and allow yourself to be constrained by it, rather than working around the protocol.

Summary

In this chapter, you explored various characteristics of a service API that must exist before you can claim you are RESTful. Remember that adherence to these characteristics doesn't automatically mean your service qualifies as a REST service; however, you can at least claim its service interface qualifies as such.

You also walked through Leonard Richardson's maturity model for REST services and used the model as a platform for comparing a RESTful service to something more SOAP- or XML-RPC in nature. This allowed you to see that SOAP services do not capitalize on various aspects of HTTP, as your REST services should.

CHAPTER 3

■ ■ ■

Designing the Sample REST API

Thus far you've learned some basic principles of the REST architecture using the HTTP protocol, and you're now ready to start working on your task-management service. But first, you'll need to take some time to carefully build up tables of resource types, their available HTTP actions, and associated URIs—similar to what you did in the last chapter with the account service example. Modeling these types will be the most important part of this exercise, similar in kind to the importance of patiently and intentionally modeling a database. It pays to think it through and get it right. And, as you walk through the different resource types, you'll begin examining some code (yeah!).

You may recall from the previous chapter that a programmer by the name of Leonard Richardson created what has become known as the Rest Maturity Model (RMM). This model defines a pathway for turning a more traditional RPC-style API into a REST-style API. As you build your sample API, using this maturity model will help you map from something most developers know—i.e., non-REST—into something new and different—i.e., REST. You will need to be on the lookout for the natural tendency to degenerate into an RPC API, thus falling back down the maturity model. I'll try to draw attention to those moments where a wrong choice could send you sliding back down.

Also in this chapter, you will model a small database for storing tasks and their supporting data. You won't spend much time doing so, as building a RESTful versus a non-RESTful service doesn't change your approach to database modeling. Either way, you need to store instances of your resources and their relationships.

Finally, you will walk through what I and many others believe to be good choices for components/frameworks in the world of .NET development right now (in the context of an MVC4 and Web API service, of course). Since you're going to build a working service application, I'll show you the best examples I can for choosing components such as an O/RM, a logger, an IoC container, and so on. Obviously, there are many options out there—both commercial and open source. The choices you'll see in this chapter are based on my own experience and those of my closest colleagues over the past 15+ years.

Task Management Resource Types

Let's start by thinking about some things you want the callers of the API to be able to do. Since this service is focused on task management, most of the capabilities it offers will be centered on creating, viewing, and updating tasks. To support these tasks, you will want to model categories, priorities, statuses, and users. All in all, this will be a pretty lightweight service. Again, a domain that is simple and well understood will allow you to focus on the non-domain concepts you're concerned about in this book. Specifically, that includes REST, ASP.NET MVC4, and the Web API.

First and foremost, the caller should be able to create a new task. And it should be able to do so without being required to provide anything more than a subject. Values such as start date, end date, priority, and so on can all be updated later if not known at the time the task is created. When creating a new task, you will have the system create its identifier—as opposed to the caller generating a custom identifier and passing it in. The caller should, of course, also be able to update or delete an existing task.

A task will need to support zero or more users as assignees of the task. Most systems dealing with tasks allow only a single user assignment, but that's always bugged me. Further, allowing multiple user assignments to a task will make the API a little more interesting.

In terms of users, you need to provide a listing of all users to the caller. For the purpose of seeing how this works, you'll allow the caller to either list them all or submit a search string. You can then use the search string against the first and last names of all users in the system. The task management example is about managing tasks, so you won't support adding, updating, or deleting users.

Finally, to support classification of the tasks, you will provide category, status, and priority values. The available values for status and priority will be set by the system, so they will only need to support a listing of all values. For categories, you will need to allow the caller to update the available values.

Figure 3-1 illustrates what the resource types will look like as a class diagram in Visual Studio 2012.

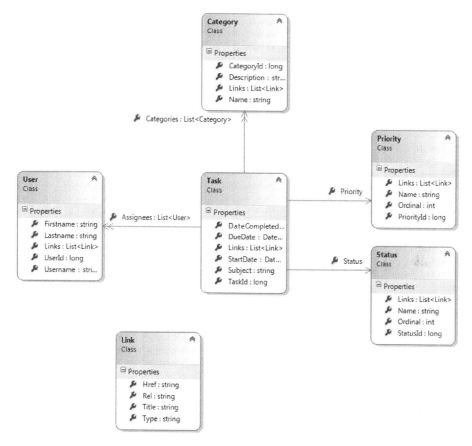

Figure 3-1. *A Class Diagram of Resource Types*

Note, however, that one of the guiding rules of the REST architecture is to avoid coupling the client to the server by sharing type definitions. So, even though you will be using classes within server code to represent the resources you receive from and send to the caller, these definitions are purely internal. This is markedly different from SOAP, where a WSDL document defines all service interfaces, methods and their signatures, and all message types very explicitly. Indeed this SOAP agreement is a contract, and it couples the client to the definitions on the server. But in REST you want to avoid this coupling as much as possible, and do your best to keep the "contractual" elements of your service constrained to those defined by the HTTP protocol (i.e., the HTTP verbs, using URIs for accessing resources, and utilizing hypermedia as the engine of application state).

Hypermedia Links

Speaking of hypermedia, you no doubt noticed the Link class in Figure 3-1, along with the associated List<Link> properties on all other classes. Remember that you want to lead the API consumer through your application—similar to the way a user in a web browser is led through a web site with various hyperlinks and web forms. As such, each and every time you send a resource representation back to the caller, you need to give it a list of available actions (i.e., state changes).

Let's look at the Link class in more detail:

```
public class Link
{
    public string Rel { get; set; }
    public string Href { get; set; }
    public string Title { get; set; }
    public string Type { get; set; }
}
```

This should look familiar to you, as it is very similar to the link HTML element. Indeed, you're trying to give the user very similar information to that provided by the link element:

- Rel: Specifies the relationship between the resource and the resource identified in the link

- Href: Specifies the linked resource's address

- Title: Specifies a title or tag for the action (e.g., Delete, Next, Update)

- Type: Specifies the MIME type of the linked resource; this is known as a "media type" in the REST world

One of the issues with using links like the one just specified is that the REST architecture doesn't define any specific standard for building hypermedia links in an API. If you search the Internet to find some semblance of a common approach, you will find many different opinions. That said, the leading candidate appears to be ATOM-style links, which look similar to the HTML link element but are intended for aggregate reader consumption.

RMM LOOKOUT

You might be tempted to use a set of more-specific links than just a collection of string-oriented link objects. For example, you could have Link properties for the following:

- Update
- Delete
- Assignees
- NewAssignment

But you need to remember that the RESTful service needs to look, act, and smell like a state machine. That means you must have resources moving through states via predefined state transitions. As defined by REST, your service must specify the allowed transitions for any given resource based on the current state of that resource. In other words, the available links (i.e., state transitions) will change from one call to the next, depending on what state you're in (e.g., the state of the Task and the permissions of the current user). Therefore, it is imperative that the list of links be dynamic.

There's another important reason for using a collection of links for the state transitions: the Single Responsibility Principle (SRP). Introduced by Robert C. Martin in 2002, the principle essentially states that a class should have only one reason to change; that is, it should only be responsible for one thing.

If you put those state transitions on your resource types, then you violate SRP because now your resource definition will need to change every time you want to change any of the available state transitions. Your definition will also change if you add to or remove any transitions. Instead, the available transitions should be dictated by a separate class–not the resource type class. In other words, the rules that decide what actions the caller is allowed to take on a given resource should be external to that resource. If you keep the available transitions loose (your collection of Link objects), then the service code doing the work of returning a resource can be the one to worry about creating appropriate links.

Before you get into modeling your resources against URIs and HTTP verbs, let's quickly look at the class code for your resource types:

```
public class Task
{
    public long TaskId { get; set; }
    public string Subject { get; set; }
    public DateTime? StartDate { get; set; }
    public DateTime? DueDate { get; set; }
    public DateTime? DateCompleted { get; set; }
    public List<Category> Categories { get; set; }
    public Priority Priority { get; set; }
    public Status Status { get; set; }
    public List<Link> Links { get; set; }
    public List<User> Assignees { get; set; }
}

public class Category
{
    public long CategoryId { get; set; }
    public string Name { get; set; }
    public string Description { get; set; }
    public List<Link> Links { get; set; }
}
```

```
public class Priority
{
    public long PriorityId { get; set; }
    public string Name { get; set; }
    public int Ordinal { get; set; }
    public List<Link> Links { get; set; }
}

public class Status
{
    public long StatusId { get; set; }
    public string Name { get; set; }
    public int Ordinal { get; set; }
    public List<Link> Links { get; set; }
}

public class User
{
    public long UserId { get; set; }
    public string Username { get; set; }
    public string Firstname { get; set; }
    public string Lastname { get; set; }
    public string Email { get; set; }
    public List<Link> Links { get; set; }
}
```

There's nothing particularly remarkable about these types, but do note that their identifiers are integers, and those identifying values will be generated by the service, not provided by the caller. Also note that the Task can have zero or more Category instances associated with it.

Modeling the URIs and HTTP Verbs

Just as you did in Chapter 2 with the account service, you now want to model each resource type's allowed HTTP verbs and associated URIs. The operations (i.e., verbs) available will vary from type to type—you aren't required to support all of the verbs on each resource type or URI.

Let's start with an easy one: Status. Table 3-1 illustrates that you want to support only two operations.

Table 3-1. *A List of Status Operations*

URI	Verb	Description
/api/statuses	GET	Gets the full list of all statuses
/api/statuses/123	GET	Gets the details for a single status

You don't need to allow the caller to modify the list of statuses, so these two GET operations are sufficient. The Priority resource type will be similar (see Table 3-2).

Table 3-2. *A List of Priority Operations*

URI	Verb	Description
/api/priorities	GET	Gets the full list of all priorities
/api/priorities/123	GET	Gets the details for a single priority

Modeling the Category resource type will be a little more complicated because you need to allow the caller to modify the list of categories (see Table 3-3).

Table 3-3. *A List of Category Operations*

URI	Verb	Description
/api/categories	GET	Gets full list of all categories
/api/categories/123	GET	Gets the details for a single category
/api/categories	PUT	Replaces the entire list of categories with the one given
/api/categories/123	PUT	Update the specified category
/api/categories	POST	Creates a new category
/api/categories	DELETE	Deletes all categories
/api/categories/123	DELETE	Deletes the specified category

At this point, I want to take a minute to point out a few things from Table 3-3. First, as you may recall from Chapter 2, you can use GET to retrieve either a single resource or a collection of resources. (Of course, this is what you're also doing for the Status and Priority resources) Notice, too, that you are using PUT in a similar manner—that is, you're updating a single category or replacing the entire list. This might be useful when first initializing the system's available categories.

Next, note that the caller will use a POST request on the Categories collection resource in order to create a new category. This is required since the category identifier (the CategoryId property) is generated by the system. If you were allowing the caller to give you the identifier, then you wouldn't need the POST method. Instead, you would just use PUT on a single resource to either create or update that particular category.

Finally, the DELETE verb is being used in two different contexts. The caller can specify a single category to delete, or it can use the collection resource URI to delete the entire list of categories.

Moving ahead, the URIs and verbs for the User resource type will be similar to the Status and Priority types. The task-management service isn't going to allow the caller to modify the list of users in the system. You'll save user management for a separate service (that you aren't going to write!). Table 3-4 illustrates the two operations you will allow on the User.

Table 3-4. *A List of User Operations*

URI	Verb	Description
/api/users	GET	Gets the full list of all users; optionally specifies a filter
/api/users/123	GET	Gets the details for a single user

The main difference between this resource type and the Status and Priority types is that you want to allow the caller to supply a filter for limiting the list of users you return. This will be in the form of URL request string arguments. You'll explore the details of user querying later, when you start building the service code.

ODATA

The /api/users URI in your task-management service will be providing limited querying and filtering capability in the way of simple wildcard-enabled search strings. And you might be tempted to allow more complex queries by supporting ANDs and ORs, parentheses, TOP, ORDERBY, and so on. However, it is for these capabilities that the Open Data Protocol (OData) exists. This protocol was created by Microsoft and a few other companies to standardize web-based data querying and updating.

Here's what the www.odata.org web site says:

> The Open Data Protocol (OData) enables the creation of REST-based data services, which allow resources, identified using Uniform Resource Identifiers (URIs) and defined in a data model, to be published and edited by Web clients using simple HTTP messages.

In fact, the ASP.NET Web API provides a simple mechanism for supporting OData with your REST service; you'll learn more about this later.

Finally, you need to define the URIs and HTTP verbs for the Task resource type. Table 3-5 shows the list of operations available for the Task.

Table 3-5. *A List of Task Operations*

URI	Verb	Description
/api/tasks	GET	Gets the full list of all tasks; optionally specify a filter
/api/tasks/123	GET	Gets the details for a single task
/api/tasks/123/status	GET	Gets just the status information for the specified task
/api/tasks/123/status/456	PUT	Updates just the status of the specified task
/api/tasks/123/priority	GET	Gets just the priority information for the specified task
/api/tasks/123/priority/456	PUT	Updates just the priority of the specified task
/api/tasks/123/users	GET	Gets the users assigned to the specified task
/api/tasks/123/users	PUT	Replaces all users on the specified task
/api/tasks/123/users	DELETE	Deletes all users from the specified task
/api/tasks/123/users/456	PUT	Adds the specified user (e.g., 456) as an assignee on the task
/api/tasks/123/users/456	DELETE	Deletes the specified user from the assignee list
/api/tasks/123/categories	GET	Gets the categories associated with the specified task
/api/tasks/123/categories	PUT	Replaces all categories on the specified task
/api/tasks/123/categories	DELETE	Deletes all categories from the specified task
/api/tasks/123/categories/456	PUT	Adds the specified category—e.g. 456—to the task
/api/tasks/123/categories/456	DELETE	Removes the specified category from the task
/api/tasks	POST	Creates a new task

Here you see something that wasn't present in the previous resource types: using PUT and DELETE on a collection of resources. In order to add a new assignee to a task, the caller utilizes the users collection, adding or deleting specific users one at a time. Or, optionally, the caller can use PUT or DELETE against the entire collection. According to the HTTP protocol, this will replace or delete all users associated with the task. The same applies to the categories associated with a given task.

Note that the status and priority values are not collections; however, you still want to allow the caller to update just the status (e.g., to set the task as complete) or just the priority.

That wraps up this chapter's exploration of designing the resource types; next, you will learn how to perform a quick modeling of the database.

The Task-Management Data Model

In this section, you're going to create your model for storing the task-management service data. As mentioned previously, you won't linger here for long. The main goal is just to keep building up your sample service, so you can get on to writing some Web API code.

Logically, you have three categories of data to store:

- Reference data

- Tasks

- Users and Roles

The reference data tables will be used to store available values for task priorities, categories, and statuses. Each of these will include an identifier, a name, and a description and/or ordinal. The ordinal value will let the database recommend the sorting preference when displaying the reference data to the user in dropdown or other list controls.

The task data is pretty straightforward, and it amounts to simply storing the task itself and its attributes. You will use a many-to-many table to link tasks to categories and users because a task can be associated with zero or more of each. However, the status and priority values will just be attributes on the task. Another many-to-many table will be used to assign a task to zero or more users.

Figure 3-2 shows the database tables of the reference and task data, including their associated link tables. Note that this particular diagram excludes the tables storing most of the information for users and roles—you'll learn about that next.

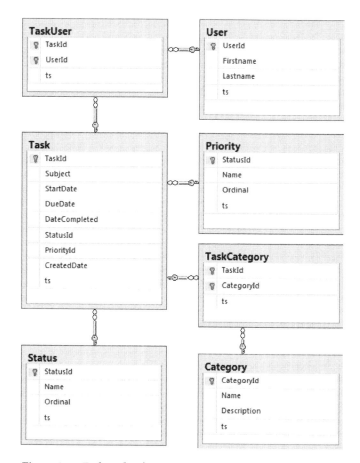

Figure 3-2. *Task and Reference Data Tables*

Most of the model in Figure 3-2 looks similar to the resource types you designed earlier in this chapter. However, this model includes a column called ts for each table. As a matter of practice, it is a good idea to include a versioning column to be used for concurrency checking (i.e., checking for dirty data on update). I chose ts for the column name for a few reasons: it stands for *timestamp*, it's short, and it typically doesn't conflict with other column names.

In SQL Server, you can use the rowversion data type; SQL Server will automatically update a rowversion column every time a row is added or updated. The non-nullable rowversion type is equivalent to an 8-byte binary column in terms of its underlying storage. SQL Server uses a unique incrementing binary value, scoped to the entire database, for generating the rowversion values. If you want to view the rowversion values as easier-to-read numbers, you can cast them to unsigned 64-bit integers. Every time a row in the database is added or updated, the current rowversion value will be incremented by one. Later on, as you build the code, you'll see exactly how the ts column is used to ensure proper concurrency checking.

The third category of data you need to store relates to users and their roles. For a given user, you need to include firstname and lastname, an email address, and maybe the date the user was created in your system.

You also need to store information related to authentication. This includes the login credentials (i.e., username and password), the last time the user attempted to log in, how many failed password attempts, a secret question and answer, and a flag to indicate whether a user's account is currently locked. Granted, your API design doesn't account for most of this type of data. Indeed, you didn't provide any resource types or URIs dealing with account management. However, as you'll see later, you will need to provide a mechanism for user to sign on—otherwise, you won't know who the current user is, and you won't be able to apply roles and associated permissions. As such, even if your simple API doesn't allow for user management, the underlying code and database will need to support basic user authentication and authorization.

You've likely heard it said before: "Never roll your own security architecture!" I am a firm believer in that philosophy, but occasionally you must work with legacy systems that did in fact create their security architecture from scratch. If you have any say in it, however, do *not* do the same! There are plenty of tried-and-true frameworks, tools, servers, and the like available to you that have all been designed and built by people who know way more than you or me about security. So do yourself, your company, and your client a favor, and use one of them.

The task-management service is no exception in that regard. As you'll see later, the solution illustrated in this book uses the ASP.NET Membership Provider with SQL Server to supply what you need for authentication and authorization. So in Figure 3-3, which models all of the user-related data, you will note that some of the tables have names that start with aspnet_. This is because you will use the aspnet_regsql.exe tool to generate those tables. And in the data model, you will simply link to the aspnet_Users table from the User table.

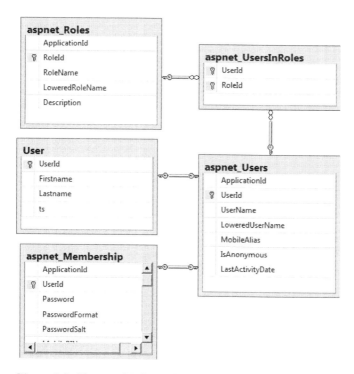

Figure 3-3. *Users and Roles in the Data Model*

While the aspnet_ tables provide all you need for authentication and authorization, they don't provide basic user information (e.g., firstname and lastname). So, as shown in the diagram, you create your own User table with these two attributes, so that has a one-to-one foreign key to the aspnet_Users table. In doing so, you can treat a user—with all the information you need—as a single entity once you pull the data from the database and into the application-based domain model. The main thing you'll need to do, in order to avoid SQL Server foreign key errors, is to use the ASP.NET Membership API to create a new user before you add the user's record in your own User table.

At this point, you've designed all of your resource types, and you've laid out the URIs and HTTP verbs for those types. You've also just briefly modeled the underlying database to be used to store your resources, as well as to provide support for user authentication and authorization. Before closing out this chapter, let's spend a bit of time choosing the various architecture components you'll need to build your service application.

Choosing Architecture Components

Now that you've done most of the high-level design of your API (including the database), it's time to explore some of the various tools and frameworks available to you in the context of an ASP.NET MVC 4 Web API REST service (that was a mouthful!). As I mentioned in the opening of this chapter, my selections are based on my own experience and those of some of my closest colleagues over the years. In no way do I mean to advocate any one tool over any other all of the time—"it depends" is one of the best answers any architect can give when asked to comment on tool recommendations. It would be foolish of anyone to say that you must *always* choose a certain tool because so much of an application's context and existing architecture can inform such decisions.

That said, I've been working in the world of .NET services for many years. And while I can't claim I've tried or used all of the framework-level tools out there, I feel comfortable saying I've used most of the major ones both experimentally and in the context of professional enterprise applications. Further, this work hasn't been in a vacuum. Like any good software engineer, I've leaned heavily on the experience of those around me. This includes both people from the Internet and trusted colleagues with whom I've worked closely on projects.

The purpose of this book is to take you from a near-zero level of experience in writing .NET services; teach you about REST, MVC 4, and the Web API; and have you end up with a fully functional REST-style service. As such, I feel it prudent to share my experiences and opinions regarding these framework and tools—for the purpose of making sure you don't try to build a service without utilizing components already available to you. I've watched way too many developers create their own logger or their own authentication code. If these tools are new to you—or if even the thought that you should look at them in the first place is new—then I encourage you to read this section carefully. I also encourage you to follow up with your own research and experimentation.

However, if you are a seasoned developer who's been down this path many times, then I think it's best that you read enough to at least understand the code. I certainly don't intend to persuade you into abandoning what you've found to work well. And, in most cases, adapting the code to use your choice of tool wouldn't take much work, anyway.

OK, one more kick to this dead horse: rather than attempt to create an in-depth review of all of the pros and cons for each tool and its alternatives, I've decided to write this section as if you and I were casually sharing opinions over coffee. So take this section with a grain of salt and remember that my main intent here is to make sure you feel comfortable in your tool selection when building these services.

Here's a list of the types of components this section will look at:

- Data access / ORM
- IoC container
- Logger
- Authentication and authorization
- Testing framework
- Mocking framework
- Build and deployment scripting

Data Access

There are quite a few options available in .NET when it comes to data access and object persistence on SQL Server. Most of these options fall into one of two categories: using the various SqlClient objects (e.g., SqlConnection, SqlDataAdapter, and SqlCommand) with stored procedures or embedded SQL; or using an Object Relational Mapper (ORM). Sometimes the two approaches are used together, but more often developers choose one or the other.

What I've found to work best most the time, on applications where the database schema isn't too crazy (and there isn't any requirement to squeeze every last ounce out of performance), is to use *NHibernate* for most of the basic Create-Read-Update-Delete (CRUD) work—and then supplement that with stored procedure calls, as needed. The separation between the Unit of Work object (i.e., the ISession) and your repository objects is the main benefit, in my opinion. This is especially the case within web or service applications, where you want a given call to execute within the context of a single database session and transaction.

NHibernate is particularly well-suited for this scenario; in fact, it comes with built-in support for associating Unit of Work instances with ASP.NET or WCF call contexts. This benefit allows the developer to configure the lifetime and injection of ISession objects just once—and then never have to mess with them again. As you'll see, using an IoC container along with NHibernate and its link with ASP.NET allows for near-transparent yet very reliable database-transaction management.

UNIT OF WORK AND REPOSITORY PATTERNS

Martin Fowler introduces some extremely valuable enterprise patterns in his book, *Patterns of Enterprise Application Architecture* (Addison-Wesley, 2002). If you aren't familiar with the definition and use-cases of Unit of Work and Repository as they apply to data access, then I strongly encourage you to read up on them in Martin's book. For a free and quick summary of the patterns, you can also visit www.martinfowler.com, where he offers some brief descriptions and diagrams of some of the patterns found in the book. Possessing a solid understanding of such data access–related patterns is key to properly managing database connections and transactions, in-memory object state, data cache. It is also critical to maintaining testability.

As you work with NHibernate in your task management sample REST service, be sure to note the way in which the code manages the lifetime and injection of ISession instances. This is arguably the key to much of the value of using NHibernate within ASP.NET MVC applications. Also, if you use NHibernate and maintain a separation of the data model classes from the actual repositories and mapping files, then you can create a true provider-agnostic data access interface layer. I'm a huge fan of code and architecture cleanliness and simplicity, so the fact that you can completely separate the caller from anything SQL Server–related is a very important to me (even if I never intend to support any other platform beyond SQL Server).

IoC Container

These days, whether working in .NET or in Java, not using an IoC container of some sort can almost be considered foolish. Again, there are certainly special circumstances that might require you to manage dependencies yourself. But generally speaking, using one of the available frameworks is pretty much a no-brainer. If you're one of the many developers who don't know what an IoC container is used for, I suspect this method of managing dependencies and using such a tool might be the most valuable thing you will learn from this book. Seriously, dependency injection tends to be the anchor on which most other good patterns and practices hang.

I've used a few different IoC containers, and the one I like best is *Ninject*. It is extremely simple to use, contained within a single DLL, and configured with a fluent-like syntax (e.g., when registering the various type mappings and object instances). It also has the ability to register a callback method for type resolution, which will come in handy when you want to make NHibernate ISession objects available for constructor injection into your repository objects.

Logger

If you ask 10 people for their opinion on the best logger, you will likely get 11 different answers. There are many ways to write log messages from within an application, including built-in .NET tracing. What's most important with loggers is that you can configure them via configuration files—*not* by changing code and recompiling. As such, any logger worth considering will offer some degree of the following capabilities—all configurable at runtime (or during deployment):

- Filtering

- Log levels

- Routing

- Formatting

Filtering allows you to write code using certain tags or categories, and then filter them out at runtime. For example, a filter value might be a certain section of the application called authentication, or a certain class called Mvc4ServicesBook.Web.Api.TasksController. So the code itself would have this category either hard-coded or inserted by the logger, and then the configuration file could be used to turn those categories on or off. In this manner, you can decide at run time to log certain types of messages. Obviously, you don't want to be required to update and recompile your code in order to log more information.

Log levels are essentially a special case of filtering, where the different log levels are typically DEBUG, VERBOSE, INFO, WARNING, ERROR, CRITICAL, and FATAL (or some combination thereof). This particular filter is used often enough that most loggers make it a prominent part of the API. For example, *log4net*'s logger class contains methods named after those levels: Debug(), Verbose(), Info(), and Error().

Routing describes the ability for log messages to be sent to different targets by simply updating the configuration file. In other words, the code itself knows nothing about where the log data will eventually end up—it just sends log messages to the logger. Then, at deployment or runtime, the configuration file is updated to route log data to one or more providers. Examples of some providers include text file, XML file, Windows event log, SMTP server/e-mail, and SQL Server databases. Typically, you can also configure different routes for different filters, as in these examples:

- Send info and debug messages to a log file

- Send warning and error messages to the event log

- Send fatal messages to an ops team via email

Again, these types of routes and filters should be updatable via updates to a configuration file.

Finally, a logger should offer the ability to use format strings for log messages. This means that—again, via the configuration file—you can tell the logger exactly how you want the log messages to look. These log format strings are usually similar to what you might use when specifying the format string in a call to the .NET function, String.Format(). Further, it should be possible to utilize predefined tokens for logger-provided pieces of information. For example, the following should be available to you: the current date and time (including the ability to specify a date/time format string), logger name, ThreadId, log level, currently executing method, class name, and so on. Here's an example from log4net:

```
%date %-5level [%thread] %logger - %message%newline%exception
```

My logger of choice has been log4net for quite a while now. Beyond the capabilities I just described, log4net's logger is an ILog interface. This means you can use dependency injection for supplying logger instances to any class in the application. Some loggers (e.g., Microsoft's Enterprise Application Library Logging Block) don't offer an interface-based logger. So you either have to wrap the entire logging API with an adapter; or, you are forced to statically bind your class code to a specific logger. At least, that was my experience.

Bottom line: The log4net logging framework is simple to use, provides a logger interface that can be used with IoC containers, comes with numerous options for routing and filtering, and has been used all around the world in thousands of .NET applications for many years.

Authentication and Authorization

As mentioned previously, security infrastructure is not something you should be building from scratch. When it comes to ASP.NET applications, one of the most accessible options available is the *ASP.NET Membership Provider*. It provides support for managing users, logging on (i.e., validation credentials), password fail attempts, locked accounts, a secret question and answer, and multiple data stores for user information. For example, you can choose to store your users in a SQL Server database (which is what you're doing with your task-management service) or use Windows Active Directory for authentication. You can even implement your own provider, should you already have a database of usernames and passwords that you need to maintain.

One additional benefit of the ASP.NET Membership Provider is that it integrates easily with the role-based security of pages and MVC controllers, as well as their methods. Once you have it configured, you can simply place the [Authorized] attribute on a web resource, and ASP.NET will ensure that the current user has been authorized. Optionally, the current user can be verified to be in one or more specified roles.

Testing Framework

The two most prominent testing frameworks for .NET are *MSTest* and *NUnit*. Both work very well, and both have their pros and cons. I tend to lean towards NUnit for its simplicity and full-featured `Assert` class, though MSTest also works just fine. In fact, I use JetBrain's *ReSharper* to run my tests, so I never have to interact with either of the tools' test runners, anyway.

The sample task-management service leverages NUnit for its testing framework. NUnit offers a nice fluent-like interface that makes it much easier to specify expected test results. And since I'm using ReSharper to run my tests, the quality or ease-of-use of the NUnit test runner (or lack thereof) is irrelevant.

Mocking Framework

Moq is used for the test mocking framework in the task management service. So far it is my favorite mocking framework, although admittedly I've only tried a few of other options out there. That said every single one of my colleagues that has tried Moq ends up sticking with it—mostly for its simplicity and cleanliness.

Build and Deployment Scripting

Last but not least, you need to pick your tools for building and deploying your application. Deployment is an area of software development that is very near and dear to my heart, as I find that it's an area that is often woefully misunderstood and wildly neglected. It's also the final component in creating a true agile product development process. Without a good delivery process and system, all of the cool features and needed bug fixes built by developers are simply pent-up inventory and not realizing any value to the user or customer. As such, it is crucial that features and bug fixes get reliably and frequently delivered to production without requiring lots of manual (and thus, risky) steps.

> ### CONTINOUS DELIVERY
>
> To learn about one of the newest and hottest movements to hit software development in quite some time, I recommend the book "Continuous Delivery" by Jez Humble and David Farley (Addison-Wesley, 2010). This book deals with the exciting and powerful idea that you must be able to deliver software to your customers quickly and painlessly in order to fully realize all of the value being built by developers. Jez and David deal with such concepts as build and deployment automation, a deployment pipeline, moving build artifacts through stages of the pipeline, source control tools, build tools, testing, and much more. Quite honestly, it's one of the best and most enjoyable software-related books I've read in years.

Many different tools come into play when dealing with builds and deployment. My primary tools, however, are *MSBuild* and the *MSBuild Extension Pack* (http://msbuildextensionpack.codeplex.com). MSBuild is built into the .NET Framework; so if you are installing a .NET application, you will have access to MSBuild as a deployment tool. Prior to MSBuild, many developers used NAnt. But I believe since MSBuild was introduced with Visual Studio 2005 and .NET 2.0, it has since taken over as the primary scripting tool for builds and deployments.

In addition to MSBuild, you will invariably need to reach outside the normal bounds of the scripting language and do something to the environment. For example, you might need to create a web site in IIS, or run some scripts against a SQL Server database, or install and start a Windows service. This is where the MSBuild Extension Pack comes in. It is hands-down one of the best MSBuild–based tools I've ever used. In fact, on many projects, all I need to do all of my builds and deployments is MSBuild and its associated expansion pack—nothing else. And since you only need to reference a few DLLs to use the extension pack (and MSBuild is installed with .NET), it is an easy and reliable approach for building and deploying .NET applications—especially server-side applications.

Summary

That wraps up the bulk of your exploration of the API design, including the SQL Server database and a selection of the most important components in your architecture. You also learned about the maturity model for REST introduced a few years ago by Leonard Richardson.

At this point, using the modeling technique you introduced in this chapter, you should be able to properly design just about any RESTful service, complete with resource types, URIs, and HTTP verbs. You should also have a good feel for some of the ins and outs of various tool and framework choices used in building a services application with ASP.NET MVC 4 and the Web API.

CHAPTER 4

■ ■ ■

Building the Environment and Creating the Source Tree

It's time to start working in Visual Studio! You've spent the first three chapters learning about REST and the ASP.NET MVC Framework, as well as designing your task-management service and its underlying classes and database tables. More importantly, you've spent some time modeling the resource types and URLs you want to offer for your RESTful service.

In this chapter, you'll deliberately and thoroughly walk through the process of creating the task-management source tree. This will include a specific folder structure (in Windows Explorer) and a Visual Studio 2012 solution and its projects. You will also configure some external libraries using NuGet, as well as create a few project references. You will also lay down some initial code for your data model classes, service-resource types, logging, the database, and some framework-level utility classes.

It is important to set up your source tree properly; or, rather, in a manner that allows for the benefits of separating architectural layers and components into discrete folders and projects. Think of it as the foundation on which you're going to build your "business" functionality. If done right, adding the task-management service operations and making sure they are fully testable will be simple. If done incorrectly, your service code will end up overly coupled and not conducive to clean and effective unit tests.

There is certainly more than one approach (read: more than one opinion) when it comes to arranging code in .NET. And you are more than welcome to pick and choose only parts of my approach or to interject your own preferences. Obviously, you will bring your own ideas to the table, which will influence how you view the approach you are about to see. That said, it may behoove you to simply follow along for a while, fight the urge to do it your way right away, and defer mixing in your own opinions for a bit—at least until you've got a working ASP.NET MVC 4 Web API REST service up and running. Also, the source code that accompanies this book is based on the approach in this and subsequent chapters, so it will be much easier to follow if you take it as-is.

Speaking of the source code, feel free to download it from either Apress or from the corresponding GitHub repository at https://github.com/jamiekurtz/Mvc4ServicesBook.

Let's start with a few basics that will help ensure your machine is ready for your code.

Machine Configuration

In this section, you'll learn about the software prerequisites for building your task-management service. The list is actually quite short, so this won't take long. You may be able to get everything working by using a different bunch of software or versions. The specifications listed here simply note what has been tested (i.e., what is supported if you are going to utilize the example code that accompanies this book).

Windows 7 SP1 64 bit

This book is about ASP.NET MVC 4 and the Web API. Thus, you need a version of Windows that is supported by Visual Studio 2012. That excludes Windows XP altogether. The code in this book was written on 64-bit Windows 7 with SP1 installed. My recommendation would be to follow suit.

For the web site you're going to build, you will use IIS Express during development—which is installed with Visual Studio 2012. Don't worry about needing to use the Professional Edition of Windows 7 (that supports running IIS)—unless, of course, you'd rather use IIS over IIS Express.

SQL Server 2012

As discussed in Chapter 3, your task-management service will include a simple SQL Server database. Thus, you need to have some version of SQL Server installed on your local machine. I used SQL Server 2012 Developer Edition to write this book.

In general, I like to install SQL Server as the default instance (i.e., I don't use a named instance). To run the code as-is, you will need to do the same. That said, if you use a named instance (e.g., SQLEXPRESS) you can simply update the connection string(s) before trying to run the example code.

Visual Studio 2012

Since you're working with ASP.NET MVC 4 and the Web API, you will need to install the 2012 version of Visual Studio. This code will not work with any of the previous versions.

In terms of a specific edition, I used the Ultimate Edition to write this book and its code. The Professional and Premium editions will work fine, too.

One of the main reasons for using a non-Express edition of Visual Studio is that JetBrain's ReSharper is only supported on the "full" editions. And there's no way I would ever write code without ReSharper! For this book, I used ReSharper version 7.0; I highly recommend you do the same.

RESHARPER

ReSharper is one of those tools that, once you've used it for a bit, you can't go back to writing .NET code without it. Seriously, time and time again I hear developers refusing to code without ReSharper–even to the point where they will purchase their own personal copies if their employers won't pony up. It's that good!

So if you haven't used it, I strongly encourage you to visit www.jetbrains.com and take a look–and buy it. It will save you tons of time and effort, especially if you write code according to today's best practices with regard to dependency injection, unit tests, refactoring, variable naming, and so on.

NuGet Package Manager 2.1

You will use NuGet to set up the various libraries used in your task-management service. This Visual Studio add-in allows a developer to download and add project references for third-party libraries—each with a single command in the NuGet Package Manager console (window). For example, assume you run the following command with your test project selected:

```
install-package nunit
```

This code downloads the latest version of NUnit and adds it to your source tree, as well as a reference to all necessary DLLs from within your test project.

NuGet also takes care of library dependencies automatically. For example, if the latest NUnit package required another library, it would be downloaded and referenced, as well.

This book—and the example code—takes advantage of a new feature added to NuGet version 2.1 that allows you to specify a custom folder location for the downloaded packages. As you'll see later, I like to put my libraries in a lib folder above the folder that holds the solution. By default, however, NuGet places the packages in the same folder as the solution file.

To ensure you have the 2.1 version (or greater) of the NuGet Package Manager, use the Extensions and Updates option under the Tools menu in Visual Studio. If you're starting from a clean install of Visual Studio 2012, you will likely need to click the Update button on the NuGet Package Manager extension. The version number will appear on the right-hand side when you click the extension itself.

Creating the Folder Structure

Part of the challenge of creating a source tree is making sure the top-level folder structure is created properly. That is, you want to create a set of folders and paths that allow for easy branching and merging, separation of libraries from source code from documents and other types of artifacts, and are relatively easy and fast to type on the command line. You also want the folders to just make sense (i.e., to be intuitive to any developer who must look at your code).

While no real standard exists for a source code folder structure, the folders you're going to create in this section are similar to what you can find in many of today's open source projects. The structure you'll use in this project is actually quite simple—you just want to have a root folder of some kind, with five main folders under it: build, doc, lib, setup, and src. Figure 4-1 shows what this would look like under a folder called Mvc4ServicesBook.

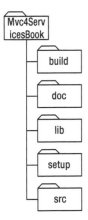

Figure 4-1. *The source tree folder structure*

A thorough discussion of branching and merging strategies is beyond the scope of this book; however, I want to point out that you will often see a top-level folder called trunk when using Subversion (or similar) as your source control repository. This is because branches are implemented with folders in Subversion, so you need a folder that represents the main line of code for your source tree. You also need a branches folder that contains folders such as v1, v2, and so on.

GIT AND SUBVERSION BRANCHES

Git and Subversion handle branches quite differently, and that might influence the folder structure you create. The sample code in this book is checked into GitHub, so it doesn't follow the conventions used with Subversion (i.e., it isn't rooted with the typical trunk folder). Git takes a different approach to managing branches. Rather than using physical folders, Git builds branches directly into the tool(s) and metadata. This means you won't have a separate folder for each branch—all code for all branches goes into the same working folder. Git handles swapping out branch content into that one working folder. If you were to check this project into a Subversion repository instead, then you would likely have a folder named trunk at the root of your source tree.

What belongs in each of the folders just described should be fairly self-explanatory. But let's leave no doubt; the following list describes the intended content for each folder:

- build: Usually contains just a build script or two, but can sometimes include supporting files (e.g., PowerShell scripts, EXEs, and the parameters file).

- doc: Contains documents related to the code base; this might include developer documents, installation guides, tips, requirements, images, and wireframes.

- lib: Contains all third-party libraries and packages used by the application(s) in this source tree; as stated previously, you will configure NuGet to place downloaded packages in this folder.

- setup: Contains the code or scripts used to deploy the application. This might be just a PowerShell, MSBuild, or NAnt script; or, it might be WiX source code or something similar.

- src: Your source code! All of the code you write for the application goes here. This folder usually contains your Visual Studio solution file(s), with all project folders being contained here.

Even though your task-management service is fairly simple and doesn't contain much in the way of application code, you will find that you still have content for the five folders described in Figure 4-1. I think you'll find that this structure makes it much easier to navigate the tree versus piling everything you have into a single folder (e.g., the Mvc4ServicesBook folder).

If you're following along and have already completed the previous section for configuring your machine, then go ahead and create the folder structure from Figure 4-1 in a path similar to this:

C:\MyProjects\MVC4ServicesBook\

At this point, you should now have a machine that contains all the software you need to build your task-management service. You should also have an empty source tree ready for creating an empty Visual Studio 2012 solution file.

Creating the Solution

You're now ready to create a blank Visual Studio solution file to which you can later add your projects. You create a blank solution first because you want the solution file to exist in the src folder. Unfortunately, Visual Studio doesn't let you create a new solution file without also creating a new folder with the same name—it's kind of a pain!

To put the solution file where you want it, follow these steps in Visual Studio:

1. Create a new solution file in the src folder by selecting Project from the File ➤ New menu.

2. Under the Installed ➤ Other Project Types ➤ Visual Studio Solutions section, select Blank Solution.

3. For this example, enter MVC4ServicesBook for the solution Name.

4. For the Location, enter the full path to the src folder you created a bit ago.

5. Click OK.

This will create a new folder and solution in your src folder. Now either close Visual Studio or just close the solution. Then, using Windows Explorer, move the new solution file out of the folder that Visual Studio just created and into the src folder. Finally, delete the now-empty folder.

At this point, you should have something like Figure 4-2 in Windows Explorer.

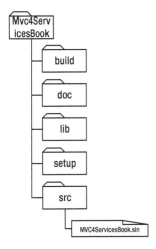

Figure 4-2. *Folders with a blank solution file*

Don't re-open the solution file quite yet; you still need to make a small tweak to the NuGet configuration for this solution.

NuGet Config File

The NuGet Package Manager was introduced in Visual Studio 2010 as a package-management system for .NET. It is similar to the Advanced Package Tool (APT) in many Linux distributions. The basic idea behind the tool is to provide a simple, reliable, and consistent mechanism for downloading libraries and their dependencies from a central repository, and then referencing them from Visual Studio projects. You will be using it to install most of the external libraries you need for your task-management service.

By default, NuGet downloads all packages to a folder called packages. This folder is created in the same folder where the solution file resides. But according to the folder structure shown in Figure 4-1, you want all of your external libraries to exist in the lib folder. As such, you need to provide NuGet with an override for the packages location.

To do this, create a new text file directly in the src folder (with Notepad or at the command line) and name this file nuget.config. Open the file and enter the following XML:

```
<settings>
    <repositoryPath>..\lib</repositoryPath>
</settings>
```

Save and close the file. Now when you open your new MVC4ServicesBook solution file, NuGet will be configured to place all downloaded libraries into your lib folder.

Adding the Projects

In this section, you'll learn how to add all of the projects to your new solution and configure their dependencies. When building an application, you wouldn't typically add all of the projects as a first step because it's usually easier to build them as you go. In this case, you'll see the more-or-less standard approach that I take when building an ASP.NET MVC-based services application, given the various libraries that have been discussed so far. This approach has been become a template of sorts for me. If you don't have such a template for an MVC and Web API based service yet, then I recommend using the structure outlined in this section as-is and tweaking it later as you get more comfortable.

Let's get started by double-clicking the new solution file (created in the previous section) to open it in Visual Studio 2012. Once open, add the projects (as the specified project types) listed in Table 4-1.

Table 4-1. *The Solution Projects*

Project Type	Project Name
Class library	MVC4ServicesBook.Common
Class library	MVC4ServicesBook.Data
Class library	MVC4ServicesBook.Data.SqlServer
Class library	MVC4ServicesBook.Web.Api.Models
Class library	MVC4ServicesBook.Web.Common
ASP.NET MVC 4 Web Application Use the Web API project template Uncheck the option to create a unit test project (you'll be using NUnit instead of MSTest)	MVC4ServicesBook.Web.Api
SQL Server Database Project (This can be found under Other Languages ➤ SQL Server.)	MVC4ServicesDb

If for some reason you don't see an option for SQL Server Database Project, you may need to install the SQL Server Data Tools. You can download these for free at http://msdn.microsoft.com/en-us/data/hh297027.

You also want to add a couple test projects to the solution. Begin by creating a new solution folder called Tests, and then add the projects listed in Table 4-2 to that folder.

Table 4-2. *The Solution Test Projects*

Project Type	Project Name
Class library	MVC4ServicesBook.Common.Tests
Class library	MVC4ServicesBook.Web.Api.Tests

Notice that you didn't add test projects for *all* the other projects. This is because not all projects have classes that need to be unit tested. For example, the MVC4ServicesBook.Data project will only contain your domain model classes and some data access interfaces, neither of which lend themselves to any kind of unit tests. You also don't have unit tests for your MVC4ServicesBook.Data.SqlServer project. It essentially contains implementations of your data access interfaces, which are just wrappers around SQL Server database calls. I generally don't take the time (or money!) to unit test database calls.

As mentioned previously, I highly recommend using JetBrains' ReSharper when developing in .NET. Running unit tests is one of the benefits of this tool. It does a great job within the IDE of letting you run individual tests or all the tests in a class, category, project, or whatever. It also completely abstracts the underlying test framework, so the experience is the same whether you're using NUnit or MSTest.

At this point, you might be wondering why you have so many projects for such a simple application. There are a plethora of reasons why this separation works well, some of which are beyond the scope of this book. The main goal here is to separate your dependencies—not require that your Common project depend on NHibernate or that you add SQL Server-specific code to anything but the Data.SqlServer project. Sure, this approach helps you during development, but it also helps you keep your deployments and updates/patches much cleaner. Table 4-3 illustrates what each project is used for and what it will contain.

Table 4-3. *The Project Usage*

Project Name	Purpose and Contents
MVC4ServicesBook.Common	Contains functionality not specific to your API or even to web services (e.g., DateTimeAdapter).
MVC4ServicesBook.Data	Contains your domain model Plain Old CLR Objects (POCOs); these are used by NHibernate to pull/push data from the database. Also contains your data access interfaces, but no implementations. Note that nothing in this project is specific to SQL Server.
MVC4ServicesBook.Data.SqlServer	Contains data access implementations, as well as your NHibernate mappings. This project is what makes the Data project SQL Server-specific at runtime.
	As you build up your services application, you should note that no code references any types in this project (i.e., the code only references the Data project).

(*continued*)

Table 4-3. (*continued*)

Project Name	Purpose and Contents
MVC4ServicesBook.Web.Api.Models	Contains your service's REST resource types (or models).
	I separate these into their own class library just to make unit testing a little easier. But remember that the client/caller never gets this DLL (i.e., you don't share resource type definitions in REST services).
MVC4ServicesBook.Web.Common	Contains functionality common to web and service applications.
MVC4ServicesBook.Web.Api	This is the REST service application itself; it is hosted by IIS at runtime. This project contains all of the Web API controllers, your MVC routes, connection string(s), and so on.
MVC4ServicesDb	Contains all the schema, code, and data for your SQL Server database. Once this project is compiled, you use the output to deploy the database to your preferred target. This works whether you want to create a new database or upgrade an existing one.
MVC4ServicesBook.Common.Tests	Unit tests for the classes in your Common project.
MVC4ServicesBook.Web.Api.Tests	Unit tests for the controllers and other classes in your Api host project.

Now that you have all of your Visual Studio projects in place, you need to add their respective external libraries and references using the NuGet Package Manager Console. These commands will download the latest versions of the libraries (if needed), and then add appropriate references to the given projects. And because in a previous section you configured NuGet to download the packages to your lib folder, you can look there after running these commands to see what was downloaded.

From within the Visual Studio 2012 IDE, open the Package Manager Console window and run the commands listed in Table 4-4. You can find the names of these packages and their corresponding install commands on the NuGet web site at www.nuget.org. Each command indicates which package to install and in which project to add the package reference.

Table 4-4. *A List of NuGet Commands*

NuGet Command
install-package nunit MVC4ServicesBook.Common.Tests
install-package nunit MVC4ServicesBook.Web.Api.Tests
install-package moq MVC4ServicesBook.Web.Api.Tests
install-package nhibernate MVC4ServicesBook.Data.SqlServer
install-package fluentnhibernate MVC4ServicesBook.Data.SqlServer
install-package log4net MVC4ServicesBook.Web.Api
install-package nhibernate MVC4ServicesBook.Web.Api
install-package fluentnhibernate MVC4ServicesBook.Web.Api
install-package ninject MVC4ServicesBook.Web.Api
install-package ninject.web.common MVC4ServicesBook.Web.Api
install-package Microsoft.AspNet.WebApi.OData -Pre MVC4ServicesBook.Web.Api
install-package log4net MVC4ServicesBook.Web.Common
install-package nhibernate MVC4ServicesBook.Web.Common
install-package ninject MVC4ServicesBook.Web.Common

You may need to add more libraries later, but this is a good start and something you can safely do on pretty much any MVC 4 Web API application.

Note that the command for referencing the Microsoft.AspNet.WebApi.OData package is specified with the -pre switch. At the time of this writing, the package was still under development. Consequently, you need to include this switch—otherwise, an error will occur. Check the NuGet web site's OData page to see if this switch is still necessary when you run these commands yourself.

If you were working on an ASP.NET MVC 3 project, you would also use NuGet to download and configure the Ninject extension identified by ninject.mvc3. Upon installation, this extension configures Ninject as the controller factory and dependency resolver for the MVC project. Unfortunately, at the time of writing, the extension wasn't yet compatible with ASP.NET MVC 4 and the Web API. This means you'll have to rely on the Ninject.Web.Common extension, which essentially links a Ninject container to HttpContext or OperationContext, enabling object lifetimes to be scoped to a single web request. But without that automatic link to the MVC controller factory, you'll need to manually wire up a Ninject-based dependency resolver. You'll see how this works in the next chapter.

Finally, let's add some project references that you already know about. More may be required later, but the ones listed in Table 4-5 are a good start. (I've omitted the first part of the projects' names—MVC4ServicesBook—so that their names will fit in the table).

Table 4-5. *Project References*

Project	References
Common.Tests	Common
Web.Api.Tests	Common
	Data
	Web.Api
	Web.Api.Models
	Web.Common
Data.SqlServer	Common
	Data
Web.Api	Common
	Data
	Web.Api
	Web.Api.Models
	Web.Common

If you've followed the steps outlined so far, you should see something similar to Figure 4-3 in the Solution Explorer for the MVC4ServicesBook solution.

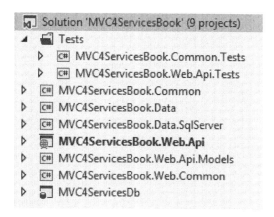

Figure 4-3. *The solution in Visual Studio 2012*

Basic Components

At this point, your solution should build successfully, even though you haven't added any real code yet. But with all the projects added and their libraries installed and referenced, you are ready to start building some of the easier components you'll need later on:

- DateTimeAdapter
- Domain model

- Service resource types (the service model)

- Logging

- Database

Let's start with a simple adapter to the .NET DateTime class.

DateTimeAdapter

I'm a firm believer in avoiding static calls at all costs—and that includes static calls against .NET Framework classes. The only place a static call should be made is within an adapter or factory class. The DateTime.Now property in .NET is a perfect example of something that seems so trivial to use, yet can get you tied up in knots many times over if you're not careful; this is especially so when it comes to writing unit tests.

Instead, you need to use the Adapter pattern, wrap the DateTime class in an appropriate injectable interface, and create a corresponding adapter implementation. Then, anytime a class needs to get the current system time, it will use dependency injection to obtain an implementation of your IDateTime interface and call Now (or, UtcNow) on it. That way, the unit test code can force the "current time" without having to resort to setting the Windows system clock during test execution.

In the MVC4ServicesBook.Common project, add the following interface and corresponding implementation:

```
public interface IDateTime
{
    DateTime UtcNow { get; }
}

public class DateTimeAdapter : IDateTime
{
    public DateTime UtcNow
    {
        get { return DateTime.UtcNow; }
    }
}
```

For the task-management service, you'll use UTC time. However, you are free to add other adapted properties, as well. Even so, this adapter is the only place in the entire code base that you see a call to DateTime.Now (or DateTime.UtcNow).

Domain Model

In this section, you're going to add your POCO classes that make up your application's domain model. These will be used primarily to query and update the database (e.g., fetch a list of users or categories and add tasks).

Since these classes will be used by NHibernate, and you want to support lazy loading, you need to make every property virtual.

■ **Note**   Lazy loading tells NHibernate to fetch related data only when it is needed – versus fetching all the data up front. For example, when a `Task` object is fetched from the database, lazy loading means that the `Task` object's assignments and categories won't be fetched until code is executed that needs those values.

Other than that, they really are POCOs. In other words, they don't derive from some special base class, nor do they return any special types for their properties. They really aren't tied to NHibernate at all, save for the virtual modifier if you want to allow lazy loading.

Next, you'll look at all the class definitions. You add them directly to the `MVC4ServicesBook.Data` project in a folder called `Model`. The namespace for all of the classes that follow is `MVC4ServicesBook.Data.Model`. Obviously, feel free to download the code instead of typing all of this in manually:

```
public class Category
{
    public virtual long CategoryId { get; set; }
    public virtual string Name { get; set; }
    public virtual string Description { get; set; }
    public virtual byte[] Version { get; set; }
}

public class Priority
{
    public virtual long PriorityId { get; set; }
    public virtual string Name { get; set; }
    public virtual int Ordinal { get; set; }
    public virtual byte[] Version { get; set; }
}

public class Status
{
    public virtual long StatusId { get; set; }
    public virtual string Name { get; set; }
    public virtual int Ordinal { get; set; }
    public virtual byte[] Version { get; set; }
}

public class Task
{
    public virtual long TaskId { get; set; }
    public virtual string Subject { get; set; }
    public virtual DateTime? StartDate { get; set; }
    public virtual DateTime? DueDate { get; set; }
    public virtual DateTime? DateCompleted
```

```
            { get; set; }
    public virtual Priority Priority { get; set; }
    public virtual Status Status { get; set; }
    public virtual byte[] Timestamp { get; set; }
    public virtual DateTime CreatedDate
            { get; set; }

    private readonly IList<User> _users =
            new List<User>();
    public virtual IList<User> Users
    {
        get { return _users; }
    }

    private readonly IList<Category> _categories =
            new List<Category>();
    public virtual IList<Category> Categories
    {
        get { return _categories; }
    }
}

public class User
{
    public virtual Guid UserId { get; set; }
    public virtual string Firstname { get; set; }
    public virtual string Lastname { get; set; }
    public virtual string Username { get; set; }
    public virtual string Email { get; set; }
    public virtual byte[] Version { get; set; }
}
```

The Version byte array property on all of the domain model classes will be used by NHibernate to detect dirty data. As you'll see later, the column in SQL Server that the Version property maps to will be of type rowversion. This value is automatically incremented by SQL Server every time a new row is added or updated in the database. In this way, you can track and detect when an update to a row will overwrite a previous update.

Service Model Types

Now let's add the classes that will make up your service model. Most of these will be pretty similar to the domain model classes you just coded, but you need to remember that your domain model classes are only used internally; that is, they are never sent to the client. That's what your service model types are used for—they represent the data that will be going back and forth between the client and your service.

All of these class definitions go right in the MVC4ServicesBook.Web.Api.Models project (they use that name as their namespace, as well):

```
public class Link
{
    public string Rel { get; set; }
    public string Href { get; set; }
    public string Title { get; set; }
    public string Type { get; set; }
}

public class Category
{
    public long CategoryId { get; set; }
    public string Name { get; set; }
    public string Description { get; set; }
    public List<Link> Links { get; set; }
}

public class Priority
{
    public long PriorityId { get; set; }
    public string Name { get; set; }
    public int Ordinal { get; set; }
    public List<Link> Links { get; set; }
}

public class Status
{
    public long StatusId { get; set; }
    public string Name { get; set; }
    public int Ordinal { get; set; }
    public List<Link> Links { get; set; }
}

public class Task
{
    public long TaskId { get; set; }
    public string Subject { get; set; }
    public DateTime? StartDate { get; set; }
    public DateTime? DueDate { get; set; }
    public DateTime? DateCompleted { get; set; }
    public List<Category> Categories { get; set; }
    public Priority Priority { get; set; }
    public Status Status { get; set; }
    public List<Link> Links { get; set; }
    public List<User> Assignees { get; set; }
}
```

```
public class User
{
    public Guid UserId { get; set; }
    public string Username { get; set; }
    public string Firstname { get; set; }
    public string Lastname { get; set; }
    public string Email { get; set; }
    public string Password { get; set; }
    public List<Link> Links { get; set; }
}
```

Recall that one of the tenets of REST is to avoid coupling the client to the server. This means you shouldn't provide the DLL containing these resource types to callers of your API. These types are there simply to make it easier for your controller code to receive and respond to such data.

Logging

In this section, you will configure your web.config file. You'll deal with initializing the log4net logger itself later, when tackling the Ninject container configuration. For now, begin by adding the following code to the Web.Api project's web.config file, near the top (and directly under the opening <configuration> tag). If the <configSections> section is already there, just add the log4net element:

```
<configSections>
  <section name="log4net" type="log4net.Config.
Log4NetConfigurationSectionHandler, log4net" />
</configSections>
```

Next, directly under the closing </appSettings> tag, add the following log4net configuration section:

```
  <log4net
xsi:noNamespaceSchemaLocation="http://csharptest.net/downloads/
schema/log4net.xsd"
    xmlns:xsi="http://www.w3.org/2001/XMLSchema-instance">
    <appender name="RollingLogFileAppender"
type="log4net.Appender.RollingFileAppender">
      <file value="MVC4ServicesBook.Web.Api.log" />
      <appendToFile value="true" />
      <rollingStyle value="Date" />
      <datePattern value=".yyyyMMdd.lo\g" />
      <maximumFileSize value="5MB" />
      <maxSizeRollBackups value="-1" />
      <countDirection value="1" />
```

```
      <layout type="log4net.Layout.PatternLayout">
        <conversionPattern value="%date %-5level
[%thread] %logger - %message%newline%exception" />
      </layout>
    </appender>
    <logger name="NHibernate">
      <level value="ERROR" />
    </logger>
    <logger name="NHibernate.SQL">
      <level value="ERROR" />
    </logger>
    <logger name="Mvc4ServicesBookWebsite">
      <level value="DEBUG" />
    </logger>
    <root>
      <level value="DEBUG" />
      <appender-ref ref="RollingLogFileAppender" />
    </root>
  </log4net>
```

There are about 101 ways to configure logging with log4net. If you want to log a target other than a rolling log file, or if you are interested in modifying the behavior just covered, you should read the log4net configuration documentation to learn more. Here are a couple of useful links:

- http://logging.apache.org/log4net/release/manual/
  configuration.html

- http://logging.apache.org/log4net/release/sdk/
  log4net.Layout.PatternLayout.html

As-is, the preceding configuration logs to a file called MVC4ServicesBook.Web.Api.log in the root of the web site; each new day will create a new log file, and it will roll over to a new file if the current file gets to be 5MB in size. This configuration also logs only errors from NHibernate (its threshold is set to log anything at a DEBUG level or greater from your own code). Typically, you would update this setting to WARN or ERROR during deployment to a production environment.

The Database

You explored the tables included in your database in Chapter 3, when you designed your service API. In this section, you will look at the SQL Server Database Project in Visual Studio 2012. However, it would require too much space to add the scripts for all stored procedures, tables, and views used in this book. So, to get the real database content, please download the source code from either Apress or from the corresponding GitHub repository at https://github.com/jamiekurtz/Mvc4ServicesBook.

To start, you will have four folders in the project—all created manually in Visual Studio (see Figure 4-4).

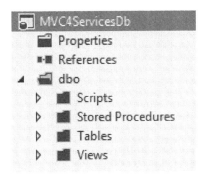

Figure 4-4. *The database project*

The scripts folder will contain your deployment scripts for adding lookup data, permissions, and optional test data. For example, you need to have INSERT statements to populate your Priority and Status values.

The Tables, Stored Procedures, and Views folders should be self-explanatory. However, you will see upon downloading the code that the project contains database objects in support of the ASP.NET Membership Provider. As always, there are a few options available when implementing authentication and authorization. This approach used in this book augments the Membership Provider tables with custom tables—as you briefly saw in Chapter 3. Additionally, the provider requires a few views and stored procedures, so you will see those in the mix, as well.

I want to point out one thing regarding lookup data: the scripts in the project will run every time they are applied to a target database. In other words, you need to be very aware of existing data—and avoid INSERT statements that will cause primary key violations. For this reason, anytime you add or update lookup data, the SQL statements need to first check that the data doesn't exist already, as in this snippet:

```
if not exists(select 1 from dbo.Priority where Name = 'Low')
    insert into dbo.Priority(Name, Ordinal) values('Low', 0);

if not exists(select 1 from dbo.Priority where Name = 'Medium')
    insert into dbo.Priority(Name, Ordinal) values('Medium', 1);

if not exists(select 1 from dbo.Priority where Name = 'High')
    insert into dbo.Priority(Name, Ordinal) values('High', 2);
```

Summary

In this chapter, you learned how to configure a clean Windows 7 machine with the software required to build your task-management REST service. You also created the folder structure you need to start adding code, libraries, and documents to the source tree. Next, you created an empty solution and added to it all of the projects you plan on using, including various library and project references. Finally, you created a bunch of basic classes and the various application configuration settings needed to support the service.

You've also added all your solution projects, installed and referenced their libraries, and added your base-line classes. At this point, your solution should build successfully. You are now ready to start creating some of the framework-level components needed to manage controller and database session lifetimes, security, and your Ninject dependency injection container.

■ ■ ■

CHAPTER 5

Controllers, Dependencies, and Managing the Database Unit of Work

It's now time to start dealing with some of the more complex concerns in the task-management service. In the previous chapter, you started with an empty folder, created a basic source-tree structure, added a new Visual Studio 2012 solution, and added the projects you know you'll need for this little REST service. You also added some of the more basic code components, and setup the project and library references you anticipated needing. While each of these things is certainly important and critical to the overall design of the service, you've yet to address any of the following:

- Controller activation

- Dependencies

- NHibernate configuration and mappings

- Database unit of work management

- Database transaction control

- Security

- Logging of service calls and exceptions

You'll learn about security and logging in a later chapter. For now you want to focus on the controllers and their dependencies, as well as working with the NHibernate ISession object and its lifetime.

Controller Activation

As you'll see throughout this chapter, services in the ASP.NET MVC Framework (including the Web API) center on the controller. You don't really have views, and the model is simply used to hold and move data around inside the application. However, the controller is used by the framework to respond to requests; it runs all of the logic the service requires. In other words, when a web request comes over the network and into IIS (or IIS Express or a self-hosted application), it uses the routes configured in your application to determine which controller should respond to the request. When the appropriate controller class is found, the MVC Framework creates an instance of that class and forwards the web request to the appropriate controller method.

Let's look at an example from the task-management service. Suppose you have the following route configured in the WebApiConfig.cs file (this is actually the default route set up by Visual Studio when you create a new Web API project):

```
config.Routes.MapHttpRoute(
    name: "DefaultApi",
    routeTemplate: "api/{controller}/{id}",
    defaults: new {id = RouteParameter.Optional});
```

Using the power of URL routing, the MVC engine will try to match the URLs of requests against this and other routes. In this particular route, MVC will use the portion of the URL specified after api/ to determine the appropriate controller to activate. Assume you were to make either of the following calls against the service:

```
/api/tasks
/api/tasks/123
```

In either case, MVC would activate the controller class called TasksController. Note that even though the URL specifies only tasks, the class name to be activated will be TasksController. By convention, MVC will automatically append the word Controller to the name taken from the URL.

At this point, you may be asking the question, "Which controller method will get invoked?" The answer depends on whether you're using the Web API. If not, the method has to be specified in the URL itself—also known as the *action*. In that case, when not using the Web API, the routes will look different—as they will need to have an {action} segment in addition to the {controller} segment. But since this is a book about the Web API, you will stick with the approach the Web API takes for method invocation.

You're using the Web API, so the URL route just shown doesn't include an {action} segment. This is because the Web API automatically invokes controller methods based on the HTTP verb the caller is using. For example, if the caller performs a GET on the URL /api/tasks, MVC (via the Web API) will invoke the Get() method on the TasksController controller class. If the caller were performing a POST instead, then MVC would invoke the Post() method on the controller.

As you can see in the preceding route configuration, there is an optional {id} segment in the URL mapping. If the caller includes some sort of identifier at the end of the URL, then MVC will invoke the corresponding method that matches a signature containing a single argument. Table 5-1 shows a few examples based on the task-management service's TasksController.

Table 5-1. *Examples of URLs and Controller Methods*

URL	Verb	Controller Method
/api/tasks	GET	Get()
/api/tasks/123	GET	Get(long id)
/api/tasks/123	DELETE	Delete(long id)
/api/tasks	POST	Post()
/api/tasks/123	PUT	Put(long id)

By default, the RESTful features of the Web API help ensure that you are coding to the HTTP verbs discussed in Chapters 2 and 3. This is much cleaner and much truer to the REST style of services than using ASP.NET MVC without the Web API. A little later, you'll see some of the other benefits of using the Web API.

In addition to using arguments that come from the URL, you can add additional arguments for data that represents your model object, as well as a .NET type called HttpRequestMessage.

Here's the signature of a Post() method that will exist on the CategoriesController:

```
Post(HttpRequestMessage request, Category category)
```

Let's examine each of these arguments.

Adding an HttpRequestMessage Argument

The HttpRequestMessage is an object that you can use to examine all kinds of properties of the incoming request. You have access to the request headers, the body, the URL used to invoke the call, client certificates, and many other valuable properties. You can also use the HttpRequestMessage object to create a response that is pre-wired to the given request object. In this Post() method, you will use it to return a response that includes the 201 HTTP response code, so you can give the caller the location (i.e., the address) of the newly created category.

Note that you could instead use the ApiController's Request property to access the same object. Since the Web API controllers all inherit from the ApiController base class, you can use this property anywhere you need within the controller code. However, you should be careful not to couple your code to anything going on in a base class. Doing so generally makes it much more difficult to test, and it increases the fragility of your code. This is why I prefer to have the request object passed into me when needed. That makes it's much easier to mock up during tests; it also means you're not coupled to the ApiController base class (not as much, at least).

COMPOSITION OVER INHERITANCE

There have been many books written in the last 10 or 15 years talking about various evolutions in the practice of object-oriented programming. One of the major shifts of the past 15 years is captured in the oft-quoted phrase, "composition over inheritance." In short, an application's code will be much less coupled—and much more testable and maintainable—if it utilizes composition of many smaller classes instead of relying on a base class for desired behaviors. When a base class is packed with a wide variety of functionality, your class—even if it's small—implicitly takes on the base class's full surface. Changes to the base class require full test regression of all classes that inherit from it—even if those classes aren't using the base functionality that was modified.

Further, relying on a base class for behaviors forces the base class to take on more than one responsibility–and this is in direct conflict with the Single Responsibility Principle. You see, if you limit a base class's responsibility (i.e., its functionality) to only one thing, but child classes require the use of more than a single behavior, then you are forced to use composition in providing these behaviors. And at that point, using a base class loses most of its intended appeal.

If the concept of "composition over inheritance" is new to you, I encourage you to read *Head First Design Patterns* by Eric Freeman et al.(O'Reilly, 2004). I think you will find its principles and presentation rather freeing, especially if you come from a strong 1990's style OO background.

Adding a Model Object Argument

The second argument, the Category object, is also inserted auto-magically by MVC. When the caller puts a JSON or XML representation of a specific model object into the body of an HTTP request, MVC will do the work of converting the textual data into an instance of that model type.

For example, if a caller submits the following JSON in the body of a POST request to /api/categories, MVC will convert the text to a Category object as the second parameter in the Post() method:

```
{"Name":"Blue","Description":"Deferred"}
```

The same applies to a PUT request where the URL also contains an identifier. Suppose you have the following CategoriesController method:

```
Put(HttpRequestMessage request, long id, Category category)
```

Now suppose the caller submits a PUT request to the following URL:

```
/api/categories/123
```

The id argument will contain 123, along with the category object from the request body, as well as the request object itself. This is quite amazing because you don't need to do any special parsing of the JSON or XML content. Nor do you need to define any data contracts, as would normally be done in a WCF-based service. In line with the more recent trend towards "convention over configuration," it just works!

Dependencies

If your controllers are going to do anything useful, they will need to use functionality brought in from other classes. An obvious example of this would be a database repository— that is, an object from which you can query the database and also save changes back to the database. Another example might be an object that represents the current user context, from which you can grab the user's name, email address, and so on. These are considered dependencies of your controller class. That is, your controller depends on them for functionality and behavior not implemented within the controller itself. And if you're following the Single Responsibility Principle, your controller class won't be doing much of anything, which means it should require at least a few external dependencies. In short, if your controller needs to do anything that isn't simply responding to a web request, then that behavior should be pushed off to a separate class and used by the controller (through composition—not inheritance!). The following list illustrates some of the kinds of behaviors that would be used by a controller (in a general sense, not necessarily in the task-management service):

- Database repository
- Financial calculators
- Transaction posting
- DateTime adapter
- File adapter
- Environment adapter
- User management class
- Validation classes
- Logger
- Cache management
- Exception wrappers

Again, the main idea is that the methods in the controllers should not be doing much more than simply using the functionality offered by various dependencies. And that brings us to the point of this section: managing dependencies within the application. Once you adopt the approach of using dependencies for most/all functionality, you need a pattern and tool for configuring and obtaining those dependencies. The easiest way to remember the overall pattern is with these two separate steps:

1. Push all dependencies up to the constructor.

2. Configure the application to use dependency injection.

Constructor Injection of Dependencies

The concept of pushing all of the dependencies up to the constructor is really quite simple, but it can be tough to grasp and put into practice for the Dependency Injection novice. Think of it this way: *a class should not use* any *behavior that does not come through the constructor*. None. Zero. Zip. This includes even seemingly harmless classes such as System.DateTime, System.IO.File, System.Environment and many other basic utility classes within the .NET Framework. It also includes the types of behaviors listed in the previous section. If your class is using anything that isn't implemented in that class, it needs to be injected in through the constructor. Period. You even want to avoid the use of static properties and methods. If your code needs to use the static DateTime.Now property, for example, you should wrap it in an injectable adapter class. You can find an example of this in this book's sample code (and also a bit later in this chapter in the DateTimeAdapter class).

A SHORT BIT ON DEPENDENCY INJECTION

The topic of Dependency Injection (DI) is quite a bit larger than space allows. There are many tools out there to facilitate DI across many technologies, and many approaches and techniques. For example, rather than using constructor injection, you can use property or method injection. For a good overview of DI, check out Martin Fowler's article from a few years ago:

http://martinfowler.com/articles/injection.html

This book simply illustrates the happy path of DI, which is quite sufficient for building just about any RESTful service with MVC 4. However, this book assumes you can look up other sources for a more in-depth education on the subject.

Suppose that in the TasksController's Post() method you want to know the current date and time, so that you can set the CreatedDate property on a newly created task. Rather than coupling yourself to the .NET DateTime class directly, you're going to use DI to inject in a DateTime adapter. This is what the constructor code (and corresponding private field) might look like:

```
private readonly IDateTime _dateTime;

public TasksController(IDateTime dateTime)
{
    _dateTime = dateTime;
}
```

The IDateTime interface, and corresponding default implementation that gets injected into the constructor (you'll look at the DI configuration in a minute), look like this:

```
public interface IDateTime
{
    DateTime UtcNow { get; }
}

public class DateTimeAdapter : IDateTime
{
    public DateTime UtcNow
    {
        get { return DateTime.UtcNow; }
    }
}
```

Somewhere in the controller code, you can then use the private _dateTime field to grab the current date and time of the system:

```
var task = new Task
            {
                // ...
                CreatedDate = _dateTime.UtcNow
            };
```

You simply follow this same pattern for all other dependencies, even for other .NET Framework classes. Another classic example is the use of Environment.MachineName. This should also be wrapped in an adapter and injected in through the constructor. Not only do you decouple the code from something outside of the application (in this case, the name of the machine you're on), but it also provides for much better testability. This is because you can now use a Mock during unit test execution and explicitly set the machine name property, as opposed to relying on the name of whatever machine the tests happen to be running on.

To summarize this section, remember that all functionality used by a class must be pushed up to the constructor as a dependency. Further, those dependencies should come in the form of an interface, whether you write it yourself (e.g., an adapter) or there is one already available for you to use (e.g., a log4net ILog interface).

Now that you've established the need and basic use of this very important pattern, let's look at how you might configure a DI tool to give you what you need at runtime.

Configuring Ninject Dependency Injection

For the task-management service, I've chosen to use the open source Ninject dependency injection tool. Ninject is easy to use and seems to be the most popular approach these days (within the .NET community). However, the same principles apply to all DI tools—you just need to account for the differences in syntax.

There are three things you need to take care of regarding Ninject in the service. The first two need to be done in any kind of application, while the third is somewhat unique to an MVC 4 Web API service. Table 5-2 briefly describes each of these three activities.

Table 5-2. *Three Ninject-related activities*

Activity	Description
Container configuration	Make sure a DI container is created during application start-up and remains in memory until the application shuts down.
Container bindings	This is where you link interfaces to concrete implementations, such as `IDateTime` ➤ `DateTimeAdapter`.
`IDependencyResolver` for Ninject	This tells MVC 4 / Web API to ask for all dependencies. This is the key that allows you to push dependencies up to the constructor on the controllers.

Container Configuration

In order for the DI container to be useful for creating objects and injecting them into constructors (as well as to control the lifetime of those objects), the container must be available for the entire duration that the application is running. In other words, a single container instance must meet three criteria:

- Be created as one of the first things that happens when the application starts up

- Be available at all times while the application is running

- Be destroyed as one of the last steps the application takes during shutdown

While it is certainly possible to wire up Ninject manually, the easiest and most reliable option for making sure the container is always available is to simply install the `Ninject.Web.Common` NuGet package. If you were following the steps in Chapter 4, then you already did this. It handles creating and destroying a container instance—within those startup and shutdown methods. All of this happens within a class that gets added to the `app_start` folder in the MVC project.

The bottom line: Installing the `Ninject.Web.Common` NuGet package is all you need to do to properly configure Ninject to work in an MVC 4 and Web API project. Pretty easy!

Container Bindings

Once the container itself is configured to be around while the application is running, you need to give it the type mappings. This is essentially just mapping interface types to implementation types—and in some cases, to implementation methods. In the previous example, where you looked at how the `IDateTime` interface is injected into the `TasksController`, the implementation would be the `DateTimeAdapter` class. This particular mappin guses Ninject and would look like this:

```
container.Bind<IDateTime>().To<DateTimeAdapter>();
```

Notice that you aren't actually creating an instance of `DateTimeAdapter`—you'll let Ninject do that for you as such instances are required.

You also need to map the log4net interface `ILog` to a specific logger. In this case, you'll create an instance of the logger and tell Ninject to use it only—and not create its own instances. This is because the log4net logger must be created a certain way using the log4net `LogManager` class. Nevertheless, registering an instance is similar to registering a type mapping, as shown here:

```
log4net.Config.XmlConfigurator.Configure();
var loggerForWebSite = LogManager.GetLogger("Mvc4ServicesBookWebsite");
container.Bind<ILog>().ToConstant(loggerForWebSite);
```

Assuming that you used the log4net `web.config` section specified in Chapter 4, the first line (where you call the log4net `Configuration` object's `Configure()` method) will read that configuration information and use it to wire up the loggers and their properties. Next, you can use the `LogManager` to get an instance of a logger—which you immediately stick into the Ninject container. Therefore all subsequent calls to `container.Get<ILog>()`—or, all constructor-injected `ILog` arguments—will use the `loggerForWebSite` instance. The main difference is that you are mapping the `ILog`interface to the logger object you created. You do this using the `ToConstant()` method on the Ninject container.

You can make all of these mappings from within the `NinjectWebCommon` class that the `Ninject.Web.Common` package adds to the app_start folder. The package installer creates a static method called `RegisterServices()` that takes the current container (called an `IKernel` in Ninject). You can use this method to make similar type mappings to those just shown. The code for the task-management service that goes along with this book includes a separate class to handle all of the type mapping. This code simply calls that class from within the stubbed `RegisterServices()` method. That class is called `NinjectConfigurator`, and it is shown in the next code snippet, with most of the mappings already present. Review the code to see how the `Configure()` method takes an `IKernel`, and then uses that to register all of the type mappings. And remember that this is called from the `RegisterServices()` method, which is called during application start-up. In short, all of these mappings are created during start-up before any of the controller methods are ever executed. As you'll see in the next section, this is important because the controllers actually need these objects to be injected into them when they are activated by MVC.

Here's the code for most of the Ninject mappings being done in the `NinjectConfigurator` class:

```
///<summary>
/// Class used to set up the Ninject DI container.
///</summary>
```

```
public class NinjectConfigurator
{
    ///<summary>
    /// Entry method used by caller to configure the given
    /// container with all of this application's
    /// dependencies. Also configures the container as this
    /// application's dependency resolver.
    ///</summary>
    public void Configure(IKernel container)
    {
        // Add all bindings/dependencies
        AddBindings(container);

        // Use the container and the NinjectDependencyResolver as
        // application's resolver
        var resolver = new NinjectDependencyResolver(container);

        GlobalConfiguration.Configuration.DependencyResolver = resolver;
    }

    ///<summary>
    /// Add all bindings/dependencies to the container
    ///</summary>
    private void AddBindings(IKernel container)
    {
        ConfigureNHibernate(container);

        ConfigureLog4net(container);

        container.Bind<IDateTime>().To<DateTimeAdapter>();
        container.Bind<IDatabaseValueParser>().To<DatabaseValueParser>();

        container.Bind<IHttpCategoryFetcher>().To<HttpCategoryFetcher>();
        container.Bind<IHttpPriorityFetcher>().To<HttpPriorityFetcher>();
        container.Bind<IHttpStatusFetcher>().To<HttpStatusFetcher>();
        container.Bind<IHttpUserFetcher>().To<HttpUserFetcher>();
        container.Bind<IHttpTaskFetcher>().To<HttpTaskFetcher>();

        container.Bind<IUserManager>().To<UserManager>();
        container.Bind<IMembershipAdapter>().To<MembershipAdapter>();
        container.Bind<ICategoryMapper>().To<CategoryMapper>();
        container.Bind<IPriorityMapper>().To<PriorityMapper>();
        container.Bind<IStatusMapper>().To<StatusMapper>();
        container.Bind<IUserMapper>().To<UserMapper>();

        container.Bind<ISqlCommandFactory>().To<SqlCommandFactory>();
        container.Bind<IUserRepository>().To<UserRepository>();
```

```
        container.Bind<IUserSession>().ToMethod(CreateUserSession).
InRequestScope();
    }

    ///<summary>
    /// Set up log4net for this application, including putting it in the
    /// given container.
    ///</summary>
    private void ConfigureLog4net(IKernel container)
    {
        log4net.Config.XmlConfigurator.Configure();
        var loggerForWebSite = LogManager.GetLogger("Mvc4ServicesBookWebsite");

        container.Bind<ILog>().ToConstant(loggerForWebSite);
    }

    ///<summary>
    /// Used to fetch the current thread's principal as
    /// an <see cref="IUserSession"/> object.
    ///</summary>
    private IUserSession CreateUserSession(IContext arg)
    {
        return new UserSession(Thread.CurrentPrincipal as GenericPrincipal);
    }

    ///<summary>
    /// Sets up NHibernate, and adds an ISessionFactory to the given
    /// container.
    ///</summary>
    private void ConfigureNHibernate(IKernel container)
    {
        // Build the NHibernate ISessionFactory object
        var sessionFactory = FluentNHibernate
            .Cfg.Fluently.Configure()
            .Database(
                MsSqlConfiguration.MsSql2008.ConnectionString(
                    c => c.FromConnectionStringWithKey("Mvc4ServicesDb")))
            .CurrentSessionContext("web")
            .Mappings(m =>
m.FluentMappings.AddFromAssemblyOf<SqlCommandFactory>())
            .BuildSessionFactory();

        // Add the ISessionFactory instance to the container
container.Bind<ISessionFactory>().ToConstant(sessionFactory);

        // Configure a resolver method to be used for creating ISession objects
container.Bind<ISession>().ToMethod(CreateSession);
    }
```

```
///<summary>
/// Method used to create instances of ISession objects
/// and bind them to the HTTP context.
///</summary>
private ISession CreateSession(IContext context)
{
    var sessionFactory = context.Kernel.Get<ISessionFactory>();
    if (!CurrentSessionContext.HasBind(sessionFactory))
    {
        // Open new ISession and bind it to the current session context
        var session = sessionFactory.OpenSession();
        CurrentSessionContext.Bind(session);
    }

    return sessionFactory.GetCurrentSession();
}
}
```

As you build the code for the task-management service—and as the code evolves over time—you will find yourself coming back to this NinjectConfigurator class over and over. This is because the classes you use for various behaviors will continue to change as the application evolves. Simply put, these mappings are not etched in stone, and you should expect to massage them as time goes on.

Now take a look at the third line in the Configure() method. This is where the code creates the dependency resolver that MVC will use to resolve all dependencies.

IDependencyResolver for Ninject

So far you've configured two things with the container:

- You configured a Ninject container instance to be available to the application during its entire lifetime. You did this by installing the Ninject.Web.Common NuGet package into the MVC project.

- You registered all of the type mappings (at least, the ones you know about so far) in the Ninject container instance with the NinjectConfigurator class that is used from the NinjectWebCommon.RegisterServices() method.

Finally, you need to tell MVC to actually use this container instance when activating the controllers. This involves two main steps:

1. Create an implementation of IDependencyResolverin which you use the Ninject container to resolve the requested dependencies.

2. Register an instance of theIDependencyResolver implementation with MVC.

Here is the NinjectDependencyResolver you will find in the example code for this book. Note that it takes an instance of a Ninject container in its constructor:

```
public class NinjectDependencyResolver : IDependencyResolver
{
    private readonly IKernel _container;

    public IKernel Container
    {
        get { return _container; }
    }

    public NinjectDependencyResolver(IKernel container)
    {
        _container = container;
    }

    public object GetService(Type serviceType)
    {
        return _container.TryGet(serviceType);
    }

    public IEnumerable<object> GetServices(Type serviceType)
    {
        return _container.GetAll(serviceType);
    }

    public IDependencyScope BeginScope()
    {
        return this;
    }

    public void Dispose()
    {
        // noop
    }
}
```

The methods to note are the GetService() and GetServices(). All you're really doing is using the Ninject container to get object instances for the requested service types. Note that, in the GetService() method, you are using the TryGet() method instead of the Get() method. This is because the NinjectDependencyResolver class will be used to resolve *all* dependencies, not just ones that you know about. Internally, the MVC Framework will be looking for other dependencies it needs (i.e., dependencies you don't even know about). Thus, you need to make sure you don't blow up if you're asked for something you haven't registered.

Once you have the IDependencyResolver class, you just need to run the following code to register it with MVC (as shown previously in the NinjectConfigurator class):

```
var resolver = new NinjectDependencyResolver(container);
GlobalConfiguration.Configuration.DependencyResolver = resolver;
```

And that's it! At this point MVC will hit the configured Ninject container instance to resolve any dependencies needed during controller activation.

NHibernate Configuration and Mappings

It's time to turn your attention to configuring NHibernate to work against the database and with the domain model classes. You'll be using the Fluent NHibernate library for both, instead of relying on XML files.

Database Configuration

As with any approach to data access, at some point you must tell the underlying framework how to connect to the database. And because NHibernate is database-provider agnostic, you must also tell it which provider you're using—and even which version of which provider. This allows NHibernate to load the appropriate driver for communicating with the database and when dynamically generating the DML (Data Manipulation Language). For example, creating a SELECT statement in SQL Server will be a little different in some cases than creating a SELECT statement in Oracle or MySQL. Indeed, one of the advantages of using an Object Relational Mapper (ORM) like NHibernate is that you can—in theory—change database providers without having to change anything about your domain model or any code that uses it.

You would, of course, need to update the NHibernate configuration and mapping definitions. It is for this reason that the data layer is separated into two projects in Visual Studio:

- One is called Data, and it is purely database-provider agnostic.

- One is specific to the provider.

The Data project includes the entire domain model (i.e., all of the classes), as well as the repository interfaces. Neither of these is dependent on a specific database provider; that is, the domain model will be the same whether you're working with SQL Server or Oracle.

The second project, named similar to Data.SqlServer or Data.Oracle, will contain the repository implementations and the domain model NHibernate mapping definitions. This approach is used because both of these will likely change when swapping out database providers.

The database configuration is generally just a small bit of code located somewhere in the application's start-up logic. Or, rather than in code, it can exist as XML in the application's config file. That means it is very easy to update this configuration, should you decide to switch from SQL Server to Oracle.

Let's take a look at the database configuration for the task-management service. Again, you're using Fluent NHibernate to make this work (instead of XML configuration files). You can find the following code in the `NinjectConfigurator` class discussed previously:

```
var sessionFactory = FluentNHibernate
    .Cfg.Fluently.Configure()
    .Database(
MsSqlConfiguration.MsSql2008.ConnectionString(
            c => c.FromConnectionStringWithKey("Mvc4ServicesDb"))
    .CurrentSessionContext("web")
    .Mappings(m => m.FluentMappings.AddFromAssemblyOf<CommonRepository>())
    .BuildSessionFactory();

container.Bind<ISessionFactory>().ToConstant(sessionFactory);
container.Bind<ISession>().ToMethod(CreateSession);
```

In the preceding code, you set four properties, and then build the `ISessionFactory` object. Let's take a closer look at those properties:

- The first property indicates that you are using SQL Server—and even that you're using version 2008 (which is compatible with 2012).

- The second property specifies the database connection string and that you want it to load from the `web.config` file's `Mvc4ServicesDb` connection string value.

- The third property tells NHibernate that you plan to use its web implementation to manage the current session object. You'll explore session management more in the next section, but it essentially lets you scope a single database session to a single web request (i.e., one database session per call).

- The fourth property tells NHibernate which assembly to use to load mappings. The `Data.SqlServer` project contains all of those mappings, so I just gave it a class name that exists in that assembly.

Finally, you call `BuildSessionFactory()`, which returns a fully configured NHibernate `ISessionFactory` instance. Next you put the `ISessionFactory` instance into the Ninject container with this statement:

```
container.Bind<ISessionFactory>().ToConstant(sessionFactory);
```

The statement that follows, where you tell Ninject how to get `ISession` objects, will be discussed in the next section. For now, just understand that you've configured NHibernate to be able to talk to the database.

Model Mapping

Next, you need to provide all of the code that will map between the domain model classes (i.e., the Plain Old CLR Objects, or POCOs) and the database's tables and columns. Depending on the database model you're trying to map—and depending on much you are trying to abstract away the model itself—building these mappings can be anywhere from very simple to very complex. The task-management service will be on the very simple end of the scale to map. This is because the database has been modeled to be exactly what you want to expose in the service, so all of the tables and columns pretty much match what the service consumer will end up seeing. However, the mapping would be more involved if you were trying to build this REST service on some legacy database that had older style table and column names, and it wasn't normalized the same way. Feel free to Google around and buy any one of several good NHibernate books if you need to go beyond the rather trivial mappings shown here. For a great getting-started guide on Fluent NHibernate, try reading the project's Wiki at https://github.com/jagregory/fluent-nhibernate/wiki.

The Mapping Classes

Since you've already gone through the model classes in Chapter 4, as well as the data model itself, these mapping definitions should be fairly self-explanatory. All of them are shown below, and I'll point out a few key things following the code. Note that all of these mapping classes are located in the Mapping folder within the MVC4ServicesBook.Data.SqlServer project:

```
public class CategoryMap : VersionedClassMap<User>
{
    public CategoryMap()
    {
        Id(x => x.CategoryId);
        Map(x => x.Name).Not.Nullable();
        Map(x => x.Description).Nullable();
    }
}

public class PriorityMap : VersionedClassMap<User>
{
    public PriorityMap()
    {
        Id(x => x.PriorityId);
        Map(x => x.Name).Not.Nullable();
        Map(x => x.Ordinal).Not.Nullable();
    }
}
```

```
public class StatusMap : VersionedClassMap<User>
{
    public StatusMap()
    {
        Id(x => x.StatusId);
        Map(x => x.Name).Not.Nullable();
        Map(x => x.Ordinal).Not.Nullable();
    }
}

public class TaskMap : VersionedClassMap<User>
{
    public TaskMap()
    {
        Id(x => x.TaskId);
        Map(x => x.Subject).Not.Nullable();
        Map(x => x.StartDate).Nullable();
        Map(x => x.DueDate).Nullable();
        Map(x => x.DateCompleted).Nullable();

        References(x => x.Status, "StatusId");
        References(x => x.Priority, "PriorityId");
        References(x => x.CreatedBy, "CreatedUserId");

        HasManyToMany(x => x.Users)
.Access.ReadOnlyPropertyThroughCamelCaseField(Prefix.Underscore)
            .Table("TaskUser")
            .ParentKeyColumn("TaskId")
            .ChildKeyColumn("UserId");

        HasManyToMany(x => x.Categories)
.Access.ReadOnlyPropertyThroughCamelCaseField(Prefix.Underscore)
            .Table("TaskCategory")
            .ParentKeyColumn("TaskId")
            .ChildKeyColumn("CategoryId");
    }
}

public class UserMap : VersionedClassMap<User>
{
    public UserMap()
    {
        Table("AllUsers");
```

```
        Id(x => x.UserId).CustomType<Guid>();
        Map(x => x.Firstname).Not.Nullable();
        Map(x => x.Lastname).Not.Nullable();
        Map(x => x.Email).Nullable();
    }
}
```

The first thing you might notice is that all of the mapping code is contained within each class's constructor. Second, notice the use of the VersionedClassMap<T> base class for each of the map classes. This custom class allows you to automatically take advantage of NHibernate's ability to check for dirty records in the database, based on a Rowversion column on each table. The definition of this base class looks like this:

```
public abstract class VersionedClassMap<T> : ClassMap<T> where T :
IVersionedModelObject
    {
        protected VersionedClassMap()
        {
Version(x => x.Version).Column("ts").CustomSqlType("Rowversion").Generated.
Always().UnsavedValue("null");
        }
    }
```

That crazy-long statement can be broken down as follows:

- Use the Version property on each domain model class.

- The database column is named ts.

- The SQL data type is a Rowversion.

- NHibernate should always let the database generate the value—as opposed to you or NHibernate supplying the value.

- Prior to a database save, the in-memory value of the Version property will just be null.

Again, all of this is to let NHibernate protect it (and you!) against trying to update dirty records (i.e., records that were updated by someone else after the data was read). Placing this statement in the constructor of the base class means it will automatically be executed by every ClassMap implementation in the Mapping folder. The IVersionedModelObject interface just ensures that the model class contains a Version property. Each of the model classes implements this interface.

The ClassMap<T> base class is defined in the Fluent NHibernate library, and it simply provides a means of configuring a model class's mapping through code (as opposed to using XML files). You do this in the mapping class's constructor. For example, the CategoryMap mapping class contains the mapping for the Category model class.

The two main ClassMap<T> methods used in the application's mapping classes are the Id() and Map() methods. The Id() method can be called only once, and it's used to tell NHibernate which property on the model class is used as the object identifier. This method also includes an overload to specify the table's key column—if it happens to not match the property name given.

The Map() method is used in a similar fashion, although not for the object's identifier. By default, NHibernate will assume the mapped column name is the same as the given property name. If it's not, a different overload can be used to specify the column name. Additionally, because this is a fluent-style interface, you can chain other property and column specifics together. For example, the UserMap class's Firstname mapping also includes a specification telling NHibernate to treat the column as *not nullable*.

You should see one ClassMap<T> implementation for each model class.

Project and File Organization

This could be confusing. To help visualize these classes, look at their file folders in Visual Studio (see Figures 5-1 and 5-2). Notice how the model classes are in the Data project, whereas the mapping classes are in the Data.SqlServer project.

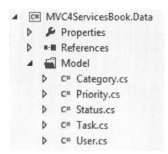

Figure 5-1. *The domain model classes*

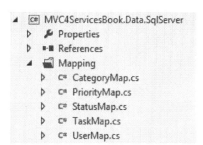

Figure 5-2. *The NHibernate mapping classes*

The Category, Priority, and Status mapping classes are pretty straightforward. They each have three properties mapped, the first of which is the class's identifier. You don't need to specify the column name because the column name happens to match the property name.

Model Relationships

The TaskMap class is a little more complicated; it contains three many-to-one references and two many-to-many relationships. The many-to-one references are simple—the task has a reference to a Status, another reference to a Priority, and another reference to a User (to track who created the task).

The many-to-many relationships are a little more complicated because you must identify the linking table in the database, as well as the linking table's parent and child columns. For example, to link a set of categories to a task, the TaskCategory table will contain a record for each category linked to that task. The categories will be loaded into the Categories collection property on the Task object.

Regarding collections, the Task class defines the Categories property like this:

```
private readonly IList<Category> _categories = new List<Category>();
public virtual IList<Category> Categories
{
    get { return _categories; }
}
```

You define the property with only a getter, to prevent the developer from replacing the entire collection. You also want to create an empty collection upon class instantiation, which allows the developer to immediately call Add() on the property without having to create a new collection first. As such, the TaskMap class defines the Categories property map with this bit of code:

```
.Access.ReadOnlyPropertyThroughCamelCaseField(Prefix.Underscore)
```

This tells NHibernate to "access the Categories read-only property through a camel-cased field that is named with an underscore prefix."

Finally, note the use of the Table() function in the UserMap class. This is used because the name of the table is actually different from the name of the model class. In fact, in this particular case, the underlying table is actually a view. The Table() function tells NHibernate to use the AllUsers view when constructing SELECT, INSERT, UPDATE, and DELETE statements. But because AllUsers is actually a database view, you will only use NHibernate to fetch users. For saving user data, you will utilize a set of stored procedures.

You do this because, for the users in the system, you are supplementing ASP.NET Membership tables with your own, so it's not a typical case of running just SELECT, INSERT, UPDATE, and DELETE statements on a single table. However, the rest of the model classes map directly to single tables, so NHibernate can be used for all SQL operations (including saving new or updated records).

Take a moment to recall the previous discussion on NHibernate configuration and the manner in which you tell NHibernate to find these mapping classes (i.e., the AddFromAssemblyOf<T>() method on the Fluent NHibernate configuration statement). NHibernate will look for and instantiate all ClassMap<T> implementations when the BuildSessionFactory() method is executed. At this point, the mapping code contained in the various constructors will run, as well.

That's it for NHibernate database configuration and model mapping. Next, you're going to look at managing the NHibernate ISession object.

Managing the Unit of Work

As discussed in Chapter 3, one of the key benefits in using NHibernate is that it allows for separation between a repository and its unit of work, the ISession object. In a service application like the task-management service, you want the database session object to span a complete service call. This provides support for three very important aspects of database class within a web request:

- Keep fetched domain objects in memory, so that they are consistent across all operations within a single web request.

- Use in-memory objects to facilitate caching.

- Track all changes made to domain objects, so that saving the changes in an ISession instance will save all changes made during a single web request; this is especially important for updates that involve foreign key relationships.

Because none of these aspects are tied to a repository or specific set of domain model classes, you can use many repositories and any of the model classes throughout a web request, as long as only one ISession instance is used. As such, it is important to ensure that every database operation within a web request uses the same ISession object. This is what is meant by "managing the unit of work."

Fortunately, NHibernate comes equipped with the ability to utilize the ASP.NET HttpContext to manage instances of ISession. In the previous section, you used the CurrentSessionContext("web") call to tell NHibernate that you intend to use the HttpContext object. Beyond that, you need to use a special class within NHibernate called the CurrentSessionContext. You can use this class to manually bind an instance of ISession to the underlying HttpContext, and then turn around and unbind it when the request is complete.

It'll be easier just to look at the code. You configure the ISession mapping with Ninject like this:

```
container.Bind<ISession>().ToMethod(CreateSession);
```

This tells Ninject to call the CreateSession() method whenever an object needs an ISession injected into its constructor (e.g., a controller or a repository). That method looks like this:

```
private ISession CreateSession(IContext context)
{
    var sessionFactory = context.Kernel.Get<ISessionFactory>();
    if (!CurrentSessionContext.HasBind(sessionFactory))
    {
        var session = sessionFactory.OpenSession();
        CurrentSessionContext.Bind(session);
    }

    return sessionFactory.GetCurrentSession();
}
```

First, you obtain an instance of the ISessionFactory that you configured during application start-up (covered in the previous section). You then use that ISessionFactory object to check whether an existing ISession object has already been bound to the CurrentSessionContext object. If not, then you open a new session (using the ISessionFactory object), and then immediately bind it to the context. (By the way, opening a session in NHibernate is somewhat similar to opening a connection to the database.) Finally, you return the currently bound ISession object.

This code will be executed every time any object requests an ISession object via Ninject (e.g., through constructor injection). This approach ensures that, for a single request, you only ever create a single ISession object. Here's an example from theUserRepository constructor:

```
private readonly ISession _session;

public UserRepository(ISession session)
{
    _session = session;
}
```

The repository can then use the injected ISession and simply assume it is active and being managed by something outside itself. In other words, the repository doesn't need to worry about session lifetime, database connections, or transactions. It just has to use the ISession to access the database and let other components take care of the rest.

To close out the ISession object, you're going to use an implementation of an MVC ActionFilterAttribute—which will decorate the controllers to ensure all calls to them are using a properly managed ISession instance. Here are the relevant parts of the custom attribute:

```
public class LoggingNHibernateSessionAttribute : ActionFilterAttribute
{
    public override void OnActionExecuted(HttpActionExecutedContext
actionExecutedContext)
    {
        EndTransaction(actionExecutedContext);
        CloseSession();
        LogException(actionExecutedContext);

LogAction(actionExecutedContext.ActionContext.ActionDescriptor, "EXITING");
    }

    private void CloseSession()
    {
        var container = GetContainer();
        var sessionFactory = container.Get<ISessionFactory>();
        if (CurrentSessionContext.HasBind(sessionFactory))
        {
            var session = sessionFactory.GetCurrentSession();
```

```
                session.Close();
                session.Dispose();

CurrentSessionContext.Unbind(sessionFactory);
        }
    }
```

You'll explore transaction control and logging in a bit. For now, let's look at the CloseSession() method that is called from the OnActionExecuted() override. Similar to the CreateSession() method just discussed, the CloseSession() method first obtains the ISessionFactory instance from the container (using a GetContainer() method that isn't shown here). It then uses that object to check whether an ISession object is currently bound to the CurrentSessionContext. If so, it obtains the ISession object with the GetCurrentSession() method, and then closes and disposes of it. Finally, you need to unbind the ISession object from the current ISessionFactory instance.

To make sure the controller methods take advantage of this "automatic" ISession disposal, you simply need to make sure they are decorated with the custom attribute, like this:

```
[LoggingNHibernateSession]
public class TasksController : ApiController
```

And then watch the magic happen!

This chapter has covered a lot of complex material pretty quickly. Thus, I strongly encourage you to read along in the example code supplied with this book.

Database Transaction Control

The last thing to cover in this chapter is transaction control for the database operations. Much as you can have a single ISession instance span all operations within a single web request, you also want to wrap all operations within a single database transaction (by default).You also don't want the controller or repository code to worry about transactions at all. It should just work!

To make this happen, you're going to use the custom attribute discussed in the previous section (where you used it to close and dispose of the ISession object). Let's look at the relevant attribute code. First, you want to override both the OnActionExecuting() and OnActionExecuted()methods. These are called by MVC before the controller action (i.e., method) is executed, and again after it is executed. Here's the code for those two methods:

```
public override void OnActionExecuting(HttpActionContext actionContext)
{
    LogAction(actionContext.ActionDescriptor, "ENTERING");
    BeginTransaction();
}

public override void OnActionExecuted(HttpActionExecutedContext
actionExecutedContext)
```

```
{
    EndTransaction(actionExecutedContext);
    CloseSession();
    LogException(actionExecutedContext);
    LogAction(actionExecutedContext.ActionContext.ActionDescriptor, "EXITING ");
}
```

Let's ignore the log-related code for now. In the OnActionExecuting()
method, you call BeginTransaction(), and then you call EndTransaction() in the
OnActionExecuted() method. The definition of those two methods is as follows:

```
public void BeginTransaction()
{
    var session = GetCurrentSession();
    if (session != null)
    {
        session.BeginTransaction();
    }
}

public void EndTransaction(HttpActionExecutedContext filterContext)
{
    var session = GetCurrentSession();
    if (session != null)
    {
        if (session.Transaction.IsActive)
        {
            if (filterContext.Exception == null)
            {
                session.Flush();
                session.Transaction.Commit();
            }
            else
            {
                session.Transaction.Rollback();
            }
        }
    }
}

private ISession GetCurrentSession()
{
    var container = GetContainer();
    var sessionFactory = container.Get<ISessionFactory>();
    var session = sessionFactory.GetCurrentSession();
    return session;
}
```

```
private IKernel GetContainer()
{
    var resolver = GlobalConfiguration.Configuration.DependencyResolver as
NinjectDependencyResolver;
    if (resolver != null)
    {
        return resolver.Container;
    }

    throw new InvalidOperationException("NinjectDependencyResolver not being
used as the MVC dependency resolver");
}
```

To begin a new transaction, you first get the current ISession object (which, thanks to the ISession management code covered in the previous section, has already been created and is accessible via the ISessionFactory object). You then use that ISession object to begin a new transaction. Pretty simple.

After the controller action is executed, the OnActionExecuted() override calls EndTransaction(). This method starts by obtaining a reference to the current ISession object. It then checks to make sure there is an active transaction—as you don't want to try to commit or rollback a non-existent transaction. If there is an active transaction, then you want to do one of two things: commit it or roll it back. This is dependent on whether an exception occurred somewhere in the execution of the controller action.

You can use the filterContext.Exception property for this check. If an exception doesn't exist, you flush the session and commit the transaction. However, if an exception does exist, you want to roll back the active transaction.

Summary

That's it for this chapter. You've finally learned about all of the key aspects of MVC Web API controllers and their dependencies, NHibernate configuration, and ISession and database transaction management.

To recap how all of this comes together at runtime, let's outline their usage with some pseudo code:

1. Caller makes a web request.

2. MVC starts activation of the appropriate controller, based on the URL routes registered at application start-up.

3. MVC uses the NinjectDependencyResolver to satisfy all of the dependencies of controller, all of the dependencies each dependency requires, and so on.

4. If any object requires an ISession object, Ninject calls the NinjectConfigurator.CreateSession() method to create the ISession instance.

5. The CreateSession() method opens a new session and binds it to the web context, so that it will be available for subsequent ISession requests.

6. MVC calls the custom attribute's OnActionExecuting() override, which in turn starts a new database transaction.

7. MVC calls the controller method, which presumably uses dependencies that were injected in during controller activation.

8. MVC calls the custom attribute's OnActionExecuted() method, which first ends (either commits or rolls back) the database transaction, and then closes and disposes of the current ISession object.

Phew! That's a lot going on for every web request! I hope you see, though, that each responsibility has been separated into small, unique classes. And most importantly, the controller and repository code don't have to worry at all about the lifetime management of ISession objects or database transactions, nor do they need to be worried about making database calls.

In the next chapter, you will complete the exploration of "framework things" by examining logging and security. And you'll see again that you can easily pull these concerns into their own classes and wire them up to happen automatically on every web request.

CHAPTER 6

■ ■ ■

Securing the Service

Ah, security. You knew you'd get here eventually. Security is one of those areas in the architecture that can become wildly complex before you know it. People are counting on you to get it right—with no margin for error. Lawsuits happen and companies go under when security is implemented poorly. You simply can't afford to mess it up!

Fortunately, because you are dealing with a RESTful service that is anchored on HTTP, you can leverage security mechanisms that have been in place for years for the more complicated and risky parts of the security architecture. And for the rest of it, you can rely on the ASP.NET Membership and Role providers. So, although some applications require volumes of documentation and source code to ensure they are secure, the same is not true for the task-management service. The implementation will be simple, and this chapter will be short.

The Main Idea

Let's start by breaking the security of the service into two parts: *authentication* and *authorization*. Authentication answers the question, "Is the caller of the API who it claims to be?" And authorization answers the question, "Is the caller allowed to do what it is trying to do?" In other words, *authentication establishes the caller's identity*, and *authorization enforces the caller's permissions*. If you recall from Chapter 5, the caller will be trying to execute a controller action.

Authentication

The first thing you need to do when the service receives a new web request is to validate the caller's credentials. That is, the caller will tell you two things: who the caller claims to be and how to validate that claim. You likely do this every day when you log into your computer (and domain) when you start work in the morning. In my case, I claim to be Jamie Kurtz, and the password I enter on the login screen validates that I am indeed who I claim to be.

Within the world of HTTP, there are several ways you can validate a caller's credentials. Table 6-1 lists the more prevalent ones.

Table 6-1. *Types of Authentication in HTTP*

Type	Description
None	You don't need to know the identity of the caller, nor do you need to protect any of the site's or service's resources by applying permissions.
Basic	The caller (e.g., a browser or an application consuming the API) adds an HTTP authorization header containing a username and password. Those values are essentially plaintext, using only base64 encoding for simple obfuscation.
	This is typically used with SSL transport security (i.e., an endpoint that exposes an HTTPS address). This protects the plaintext username and password.
Digest	Provides a fancier method of putting the username and password in the HTTP header that provides encryption for those values. This is intended to avoid the need for HTTPS.
Kerberos	Uses an authentication server, such as Windows Active Directory, to provide credential validation. This would be similar to intranet sites on Windows networks that integrate with the domain for user authentication. A lot of internal SharePoint sites use this approach so that a company's users don't have to re-enter their username and password when they visit the intranet.
Public-key, certificates	Relies on client- or caller-provided certificates to identify a user. This is not very useful in a public web site or service, but it is very appropriate for applications where the users or devices are known. An example of this approach might be an internal, portable, device-based warehousing application for tracking inventory. The group of users is relatively small and well-defined within a company's organizational structure. Each user or device is issued a certificate that identifies him (or it) on every call to your site or service.
Tokens	Largely used when third-party token issuers are involved (e.g., OpenID and Microsoft Passport). This allows someone other than you to validate a user's credentials. The caller first validates their username and password using a token issuer that you trust. Then, once the caller has that token, they use it to call your service. Since you trust that issuer, you can trust that the token securely identifies the caller—and never have to bother yourself with validating the user's credentials.

Right away, you can eliminate using tokens, certificates, and Kerberos for the task-management service. The goal is to keep this example simple and avoid relying on Active Directory or any other system for validating the callers' credentials. Those particular approaches can be overly complex and impractical when dealing with public-facing Internet applications and services. That leaves you with using digest, basic, or none. You can definitely skip none—because you do indeed need to identify the caller and enforce permissions.

Between basic and digest, basic is much easier to implement—and is sufficiently secure *as long as you utilize transport security* (e.g., SSL/TLS over HTTP—which is HTTPS and utilizes X.509 certificates for encrypting the HTTP traffic). In this way, the service application *and its callers* only have to deal with plain-text passwords; however, you can lean on the security of HTTPS to make sure those plain-text passwords are not compromised. As such, the task-management service will implement basic HTTP authentication.

ASP.NET MVC and the Web API do not ship with any tools or options for providing basic HTTP authentication against a custom data store of users. Nor do they provide any integration between basic HTTP authentication and the ASP.NET Membership provider. Therefore, you will need to build that stuff yourself.

Authorization

Once you securely identify the caller, you need to enforce some basic permissions. In the task-management service, you will have only two levels of users: Users and Administrators. For the purpose of demonstration, you will restrict the ability to modify the master list of categories to only those callers that belong to the Administrators role. All other operations will be open to all users (i.e., those in the Users role).

These days, the concept of *claims* is finally catching on. The main idea is to associate a list of key-value string pairs with an authenticated user, where the key-value pairs provide all kinds of information about the user—including the roles she belongs to. This information includes things the user is claiming to have or to be able to do, roles the user is claiming to belong to, and so on. And because a specific type of claim can support more than one instance, you can use the structure for assigning roles. Table 6-2 demonstrates what a set of claims for "Bob" might look like. Note that the Role claim type has more than one value (i.e., Bob belongs to more than one role).

Table 6-2. *An Example User's Claims*

Claim type	Example claim value
Email	bob@gmail.com
UserId	BSmith
Surname	Bob's last name: Smith
Givenname	Bob's first name: Bob
SID	Bob's security identifier; usually something issued by the system: C73832EE-3191-4DC7-A3D4-25ADDDD5496B
Role	Users
Role	Administrators

Strictly speaking, claims aren't limited to values dealing only with authorization. They do, however, provide a nice structure for adding the roles a user belongs to—which is your primary concern when it comes to authorization. You can leverage the Authorize attribute to let ASP.NET automatically check those claims when restricting a specific controller operation to a specific role.

Part of authorization is creating an instance of IPrincipal that you can associate with the current thread. Each web request executes on its own thread, so each request will execute within the context of the caller's principal. This allows all downstream code to simply check the current thread's principal for information such as current caller's ID, the caller's roles, an email address, and so on. This also allows ASP.NET to check the caller's roles before allowing a controller method to be executed. For the task-management service, you will be using the GenericPrincipal object—which is an implementation of IPrincipal—to set up the caller's identity and roles. You'll explore this subject in more detail later in this chapter.

The Authentication and Authorization Process

Each time a call comes into the task-management service, you will perform the following steps (in this order). Remember that an ASP.NET MVC Web API call is always within the context of a specific controller action (i.e., a call to a specific controller method):

1. A web request arrives that includes an HTTP authorization header containing the caller's credentials (username and password).

2. Parse out the credentials from the header—which includes converting from a base64-encoded string to a normal ASCII string.

3. Validate those credentials against the credential store.

4. Setup an IPrincipal object on the current thread that contains the current user's identity and associated claims (e.g., userId, email, firstname, lastname, and roles).

5. Let ASP.NET use the principal's claims to enforce permissions on protected controller methods (via the Authorize attribute).

Setting It Up

Now that you understand what needs to happen to secure the task-management service, let's walk through the process of setting it all up. You'll start with configuring the SqlMembershipProvider and SqlRolesProvider. These will give you everything you need to authenticate users, store their username and email address, and also associate roles with the users. These membership providers also include an API that you can use for performing security-related operations—without having to manage the database data yourself.

The membership providers also include other capabilities that you won't be using in this exercise, but which might be very useful for user-facing web applications. These capabilities include account lockouts after X number of failed login attempts, configurable amount of allowed failed attempts before lockout, secret questions and answers (used when a user forgets their password), password resets, and password complexity policies. In the task-management service, you'll mainly be using the credential validation and roles capabilities of the providers.

Make sure the following sections are included in your web.config file within the system.web element:

```
<membership>
  <providers>
    <clear />
    <add name="AspNetSqlMembershipProvider"

type="System.Web.Security.SqlMembershipProvider"
          connectionStringName="Mvc4ServicesDb"
          enablePasswordRetrieval="false"
          enablePasswordReset="true"
          requiresQuestionAndAnswer="false"
          requiresUniqueEmail="false"
          maxInvalidPasswordAttempts="5"
          minRequiredPasswordLength="6"
          minRequiredNonalphanumericCharacters="0"
          passwordAttemptWindow="10" />
  </providers>
</membership>
<roleManager enabled="true">
  <providers>
    <clear />
    <add name="AspNetSqlRoleProvider"
          type="System.Web.Security.SqlRoleProvider"
          connectionStringName="Mvc4ServicesDb" />
  </providers>
</roleManager>
```

These two sections enable the Membership and Roles classes to be used against the database within the application.

Augmenting Membership Data

The membership and role providers include their own database tables (and stored procedures and views). In order to store additional information about a user without messing with the provider tables, you will use your own User table—and create a one-to-one relationship to the membership's aspnet_Users table. The database schema for the service was covered in Chapter 3, where you learned how these tables relate to each other and the rest of the database model. Now it's time to look at how you use this hybrid data.

To start, create the database view that NHibernate will use to retrieve the service's users. In Chapter 5, you learned how to use Fluent NHibernate to map the User domain model class to the view—named AllUsers. This approach allows you to treat the membership data along with your own data from the User table as a single entity. Here's the view definition—note how it joins your User table to the ASP.NET membership tables:

```
create view dbo.[AllUsers]
as
selectu.UserId,
    u.Firstname,
    u.Lastname,
    u.ts,
    am.Email,
    au.UserName
    from dbo.aspnet_Membership am
    inner join dbo.aspnet_Users au
        on au.UserId = am.UserId
    inner join dbo.[User] u on u.UserId = au.UserId
```

This allows you to use the NHibernate session object to do a simple query for a user—by userId—like this:

```
_session.Get<User>(userId);
```

The preceding snippet returns a user object that has properties from all three tables.

The code that is provided with this book—and which can also be downloaded from GitHub at https://github.com/jamiekurtz/Mvc4ServicesBook—also includes code for saving new users. If you review the code, you will notice that some extra classes exist to allow saving user data through the Membership provider and the IUserRepository within a single operation. The API doesn't officially support saving users or user data, but the UserController includes code to enable creating test data.

You'll notice that the code includes an adapter to wrap a few of the Membership and Roles static classes. This allows you to avoid coupling the code to those methods, which would make it nearly impossible to effectively unit test the security code. The membership adapter's interface looks like this:

```
public interface IMembershipInfoProvider
{
    MembershipUserWrapper GetUser(string username);
    MembershipUserWrapper GetUser(Guid userId);
    MembershipUserWrapper CreateUser(string
username, string password, string email);
    bool ValidateUser(string username, string
password);
    string[] GetRolesForUser(string username);
}
```

And the implementation class looks like this:

```
using System;
using System.Web.Security;
```

```
public class MembershipAdapter : IMembershipInfoProvider
{
    public MembershipUserWrapper GetUser(string username)
    {
        var user = Membership.GetUser(username);
        return user == null ? null : CreateMembershipUserWrapper(user);
    }

    public MembershipUserWrapper GetUser(Guid userId)
    {
        var user = Membership.GetUser(userId);
        return CreateMembershipUserWrapper(user);
    }

    public MembershipUserWrapper
CreateMembershipUserWrapper(MembershipUser user)
    {
        if (user == null)
        {
            return null;
        }

        return new MembershipUserWrapper
                {
                    UserId =
Guid.Parse(user.ProviderUserKey.ToString()),
                    Email = user.Email,
                    Username = user.UserName
                };
    }

    public MembershipUserWrapper CreateUser(string username, string
password, string email)
    {
        var user = Membership.CreateUser(username, password, email);
        return CreateMembershipUserWrapper(user);
    }

    public bool ValidateUser(string username, string password)
    {
        return Membership.ValidateUser(username, password);
    }

    public string[] GetRolesForUser(string username)
    {
        return Roles.GetRolesForUser(username);
    }
}
```

The MembershipUserWrapper class is another adapter of sorts that allows you to work with user data without being coupled to the Membership Provider's User object—which is much heavier than just some user data. So, instead of returning the provider's User object and breaking the encapsulation, you provide an IMembershipInfoProvider interface, which shields you from the underlying Membership API.

The Message Handler

Next, you'll use the membership adapter in what's called a *message handler*. You can use handlers to intercept calls to Web API controllers. In this case, you're going to use the handler to validate the credentials of the caller (i.e., authenticate the caller). This also gives you a nice place within which you can set up the current thread's principal object.

Let's walk through the handler class one section at time. First, the handler subclasses what's called a DelegatingHandler—which is the base class provided by Web API to allow for easy implementation of a message handler. In the code that follows, note the class' base class, as well as the SendAsync() override:

```
public class BasicAuthenticationMessageHandler : DelegatingHandler
{
    public const string BasicScheme = "Basic";
    public const string
ChallengeAuthenticationHeaderName = "WWW-Authenticate";
    public const char AuthorizationHeaderSeparator = ':';

    private readonly IMembershipInfoProvider_membershipAdapter;
    private readonly ISessionFactory_sessionFactory;

    public
BasicAuthenticationMessageHandler(IMembershipInfoProvider membershipAdapter,
ISessionFactory sessionFactory)
    {
        _membershipAdapter = membershipAdapter;
        _sessionFactory = sessionFactory;
    }

    protected override Task<HttpResponseMessage> SendAsync
(HttpRequestMessage request, CancellationToken cancellationToken)
    { ....
```

You will use the IMembershipInfoProvider and ISessionFactory classes to validate the caller's credentials and then look up their user information.

Next, the SendAsync() method (part of which is shown in the next snippet) does some basic validation to make sure the web request's header contains the expected Basic authorization information:

```
var authHeader = request.Headers.Authorization;
if (authHeader == null)
{
    return CreateUnauthorizedResponse();
}

if (authHeader.Scheme != BasicScheme)
{
    return CreateUnauthorizedResponse();
}
```

The CreateUnauthorizedResponse() method looks like what is shown in the following snippet. Its purpose is to create a 401 HTTP response—letting the caller know that it needs to provide appropriate credentials:

```
private Task<HttpResponseMessage> CreateUnauthorizedResponse()
{
    var response = new HttpResponseMessage(HttpStatusCode.Unauthorized);

    response.Headers.Add(ChallengeAuthenticationHeaderName, BasicScheme);

    var taskCompletionSource = new TaskCompletionSource<HttpResponseMessage>();
    taskCompletionSource.SetResult(response);
    return taskCompletionSource.Task;
}
```

Note that you need to add the challenge header to the response. Putting "WWW-Authenticate: Basic" in a response header tells the calling browser or other application that you are expecting basic authentication credentials—and you didn't get them.

Moving along in the SendAsync() method, the next thing you're going to do is parse out the credentials from the authentication header:

```
var encodedCredentials = authHeader.Parameter;
var credentialBytes = Convert.FromBase64String(encodedCredentials);
var credentials = Encoding.ASCII.GetString(credentialBytes);
var credentialParts = credentials.Split(AuthorizationHeaderSeparator);

if(credentialParts.Length != 2)
{
    return CreateUnauthorizedResponse();
}

var username = credentialParts[0].Trim();
var password = credentialParts[1].Trim();
```

Now that you have the caller's username and password, you can use the IMembershipInfoProvider interface to validate those credentials:

```
if (!_membershipAdapter.ValidateUser(username, password))
{
    return CreateUnauthorizedResponse();
}

SetPrincipal(username);
```

The ValidateUser() method will use the adapter's underlying static Membership.ValidateUser() API call to validate the submitted username and password. If those credentials aren't valid, you want to return a 401 HTTP response—as discussed previously. If the credentials are valid, then the last thing you need to do is set the current thread up with a principal that represents the caller:

```
private void SetPrincipal(string username)
{
    var roles = _membershipAdapter.GetRolesForUser(username);
    var user = _membershipAdapter.GetUser(username);

    User modelUser;
    using(var session = _sessionFactory.OpenSession())
    {
        modelUser = session.Get<User>(user.UserId);
    }

    var identity = CreateIdentity(user.Username, modelUser);

    var principal = new GenericPrincipal(identity, roles);
    Thread.CurrentPrincipal = principal;

    if (HttpContext.Current != null)
    {
        HttpContext.Current.User = principal;
    }
}
```

Note that, if the HttpContext.Current property is null, you don't need to set its User property.

In this SetPrincipal()method, you use the IMembershipInfoProvider to fetch the roles for the now-authenticated user. You also need to use the adapter to fetch the user itself from the Membership data, in order to have the user's UserId. You can then use the UserId (and an NHibernate ISession object) to get a corresponding User object.

The User object is given to another method to create a new GenericIdentity object (including all of the user's claims). Here's the CreateIdentity() method:

```
private GenericIdentity CreateIdentity(string username, User modelUser)
{
    var identity = new GenericIdentity(username, BasicScheme);
    identity.AddClaim(new Claim(ClaimTypes.Sid, modelUser.UserId.ToString()));
    identity.AddClaim(new Claim(ClaimTypes.GivenName, modelUser.Firstname));
    identity.AddClaim(new Claim(ClaimTypes.Surname, modelUser.Lastname));
    identity.AddClaim(new Claim(ClaimTypes.Email, modelUser.Email));
    return identity;
}
```

The preceding method shows how to convert user properties into claims that are added to the new identity object. Shortly, you'll see how these claims are used whenever controller code needs any of the claim values (e.g., the current user's UserId or email address).

Finally, you use the new identity object to create a new GenericPrincipal, and then assign it the thread's current principal and to the HttpContext object's User property.

If you glance back to the five steps outlined at the end of the previous section, you'll note that you have just completed steps one through four. You now have a fully authenticated user, and their roles are associated with the current thread's principal. This will allow you to decorate controllers and controller methods with the Authorize attribute. This attribute looks at the current thread for an IPrincipal object, from which it can determine a user's roles. Here's an example of how you will use the attribute to protect the Post() method on the CategoriesController class, since you only want to allow administrators to add new categories:

```
[Authorize(Roles = "Administrators")]
public HttpResponseMessage Post(HttpRequestMessage
request, Category category)
```

The last step is to make sure you add your BasicAuthenticationMessageHandler class to the current application's message handler pipeline. You do this only once during startup, so it makes the most sense to utilize the RegisterServices() method of the NinjectWebCommon class. The code looks like this:

```
private static void RegisterServices(IKernel kernel)
{
    var containerConfigurator = new NinjectConfigurator();
    containerConfigurator.Configure(kernel);

GlobalConfiguration.Configuration.MessageHandlers.Add
(kernel.Get<BasicAuthenticationMessageHandler>());
}
```

First, you configure the Ninject container, as discussed in Chapter 5. Next, you use the container to get an instance of the message handler, and add it to the MessageHandlers collection of the Web API global configuration object. Once that's complete, all calls to any controller method within the task-management service will be intercepted by the BasicAuthenticationMessageHandler, which will validate the caller's credentials and setup a corresponding principal.

IUserSession

In this last section, you will learn about a small helper class that will represent the current caller. Sure, in the previous section, you went through the trouble of validating the caller's credentials and creating a GenericPrincipal object. However, to keep your code a little cleaner, you might prefer to use a separate interface and class that can be injected into controllers when you need information about the current user.

The code for the IUserSession interface is quite simple, as it exposes only what you need to know about a user:

```
public interface IUserSession
{
    Guid UserId { get; }
    string Firstname { get; }
    string Lastname { get; }
    string Username { get; }
    string Email { get; }
}
```

And now you can create an implementation of this interface that takes a ClaimsPrincipal (which GenericPrincipal derives from) in its constructor:

```
public class UserSession : IUserSession
{
    public UserSession(ClaimsPrincipal principal)
    {
        UserId = Guid.Parse(principal.FindFirst(ClaimTypes.Sid).Value);
        Firstname = principal.FindFirst(ClaimTypes.GivenName).Value;
        Lastname = principal.FindFirst(ClaimTypes.Surname).Value;
        Username = principal.FindFirst(ClaimTypes.Name).Value;
        Email = principal.FindFirst(ClaimTypes.Email).Value;
    }

    public Guid UserId { get; private set; }
    public string Firstname { get; private set; }
    public string Lastname { get; private set; }
    public string Username { get; private set; }
    public string Email { get; private set; }
}
```

These days, more and more online applications are using the email address as the user's username. If this is the case in your application, you may want to populate the Username and Email values from a single claim (e.g., the Email claim).

Notice how this code uses the claims from the principal and copies their values to the IUserSession properties.

To complete the configuration of IUserSession and UserSession, you need to tell Ninject how to get an instance of the interface. Back in the NinjectConfigurator class (that you learned about in Chapter 5), add the following container binding:

```
container.Bind<IUserSession>().ToMethod(CreateUserSession).InRequestScope();
```

Next, add this corresponding CreateUserSession()method:

```
private IUserSession CreateUserSession(IContext arg)
{
    return new UserSession(Thread.CurrentPrincipal as GenericPrincipal);
}
```

Remember that, by the time a controller is activated and the Ninject container is queried for anything, you have already authenticated the user and set up a principal object on the current thread. The preceding code simply tells Ninject to let you convert the GenericPrincipal that you put on the current thread into a new IUserSession object—and then keep it around for the duration of the current web request. All of this makes it possible for a class like the TasksController to have an IUserSession injected into it:

```
private readonly ICommonRepository _commonRepository;
private readonly IHttpTaskFetcher _taskFetcher;
private readonly IUserSession _userSession;

public TasksController(
    ICommonRepository commonRepository,
    IHttpTaskFetcher taskFetcher,
    IUserSession userSession)
{
    _commonRepository = commonRepository;
    _taskFetcher = taskFetcher;
    _userSession = userSession;
}
```

Summary

Well, you made it through security. By now you should have a pretty good idea how authentication and authorization can be implemented in a Web API application in ASP.NET MVC 4, including how to leverage the ASP.NET Membership and Role providers.

At this point in the book, you've learned pretty much all of the framework-level gunk that you need to. In the next chapter, you will finally build some Web API controllers using the various components you've configured and built so far.

CHAPTER 7

■ ■ ■

Putting It All Together

It's almost time to start writing the Web API–based controllers for the RESTful task-management service. You've spent the bulk of this book so far laying down important fundamentals. I'm a firm believer in *really* understanding how different pieces of an application work, as well as in knowing why you've made certain architectural decisions along the way. Essentially, you should be able to defend the choices you make for framework-level components, for the tools you use, for your application's class structure, and for the way you write all the code. As such, it's important to spend the necessary time to plan such fundamentals properly. At a minimum, you should be able to defend your own MVC 4 and Web API REST services.

A Quick Recap

Let's recap the gist of what has been covered so far. Chapter 1 introduced ASP.NET MVC as a great framework for building RESTful services. It also briefly discussed the value that the Web API brings to MVC 4, making it much easier and faster to build even more flexible and robust REST services.

Chapter 2 walked you through the basics of the REST architecture—specifically, it explained how to build RPC–style services that use SOAP. It also covered the REST maturity model in a way that helped you map from those RPC services to something more reflective of the REST architecture. For example, it walked you through several important subjects:

- The important of resource types

- Using unique URIs for all resources

- Utilizing HTTP verbs and response codes

- Leveraging hypermedia as the application's engine of state (i.e., using links to let the API consumer navigate the domain of resources)

In Chapter 3, you used the knowledge of REST you'd developed to model the task-management service's API. Essentially, you ended up with what might typically fall out of a design session for a web service: the public API specification, the data model to support the service, and a selection of framework-level components and tools. It's important to remember that the API specification, with its tables of URLs and HTTP verbs and resource types, is markedly different from an RPC design centered on SOAP messages and methods. Every resource in the domain (i.e., in the database) has a unique URL. Further, consumers of the API can alter the state of the data by submitting HTTP requests (i.e., PUT, POST, and DELETE) to those URLs. Again, this is a much different approach than using a SOAP-based API, where all operations would be POST requests of XML messages to a single URL.

In Chapter 4, you cranked up Visual Studio 2012 and created your application's solution and a half-dozen or so projects. You configured a bunch of project references and also used NuGet to install and reference the libraries you selected in Chapter 3. Next, you rounded out the chapter by writing some of the basic classes and configuration for the domain model, the API's resource types, the database, and the log4net configuration sections in the web.config file. Bottom line: At the end of Chapter 4, you didn't have anything functioning yet within the service, but you had modeled all of the types and structures that would hold and communicate data—both within the application and to and from callers of the API.

Chapter 5 was all about stitching together the various architecture components you decided to use. The modeling you did in Chapter 4 was purely about data. In Chapter 5, however, the application finally started coming alive. For example, you configured the Ninject dependency-injection container, managed the database unit of work and transactions, and stepped through the exact steps taken by ASP.NET MVC 4 and the Web API whenever a caller submits a request to one of the REST URLs (i.e., the controller methods). So, while you still hadn't built any controllers yet, it was probably clear by this point how all of these pieces would come together at runtime. Of course, at that point the service was not yet secured, and you still had no way of knowing *who* was calling the service. A key take-away from Chapter 5 was to remember to *always push all of your dependencies up to the class constructor*.

Security was tackled in Chapter 6, with an emphasis on keeping it simple. For example, you leveraged HTTP and the ASP.NET Membership provider to provide authentication, and also leveraged the ASP.NET Role provider for authorization. All you really needed to do was make sure that stuff was plugged into the Web API request pipeline—in the way of a message handler. Once that was wired up, the service was protected from unknown callers, controller methods were able to be constrained to users with certain permissions, and you could easily get information about the current caller from anywhere in the code.

In this chapter, you will bring all of this information together to build some Web API controllers. This will be the last step in finally enabling you to call the task-management service from a browser, from a web-debugging tool like Fiddler, or from any other application that can send HTTP requests.

So let's get started!

The Reference Data Controllers

In this section, you're going to create the controllers needed to finish the parts of the API (from Chapter 3) that allow the caller to fetch (and sometimes update) priorities, statuses, and categories for tasks.

Remember that the WebApiConfig class contains the default route:

```
config.Routes.MapHttpRoute(
    name: "DefaultApi",
    routeTemplate: "api/{controller}/{id}",
    defaults: new {id = RouteParameter.Optional});
```

This route will cover the URLs that deal with operations on the reference data.

The PrioritiesController

Let's look first at the PrioritiesController, as it's probably the simplest of them all:

```
[LoggingNHibernateSessions]
public class PrioritiesController : ApiController
{
    private readonly ISession _session;
    private readonly IPriorityMapper _priorityMapper;
    private readonly IHttpPriorityFetcher _priorityFetcher;

    public PrioritiesController(
        ISession session,
        IPriorityMapper priorityMapper,
        IHttpPriorityFetcher priorityFetcher)
    {
        _session = session;
        _priorityMapper = priorityMapper;
        _priorityFetcher = priorityFetcher;
    }

    public IEnumerable<Priority>Get()
    {
        return _session
            .QueryOver<Data.Model.Priority>()
            .List()
            .Select(_priorityMapper.CreatePriority);
    }

    public Priority Get(long id)
    {
        var priority = _priorityFetcher.GetPriority(id);
        return _priorityMapper.CreatePriority(priority);
    }
}
```

The first thing to notice in the PrioritiesController is the three dependencies: ISession, IPriorityMapper, and IHttpPriorityFetcher. You've already learned about ISession from NHibernate—it will be used to fetch all of the priorities from the database. The other two dependencies are new.

The IPriorityMapper was created to map between the Priority domain model type (i.e., the class used by NHibernate when fetching data from the database) and the Priority resource type that is used to send data back to the caller. The example in this book moves this functionality into a separate class in order to maintain SRP in the PrioritiesController, as well as to allow that functionality to be reused elsewhere (which it will be shortly). Here's the code for the IPriorityMapper interface:

```
public interface IPriorityMapper
{
    Priority CreatePriority(Data.Model.Priority priority);
}
```

Pretty simple! And now here's the code for its implementation:

```
public class PriorityMapper : IPriorityMapper
{
    public Priority CreatePriority(Data.Model.Priority priority)
    {
            return new Priority
                    {
                        PriorityId = priority.PriorityId,
                        Ordinal = priority.Ordinal,
                        Name = priority.Name,
                        Links = new List<Link>
                                {
                                    new Link
                                        {
                                            Title = "self",
                                            Rel = "self",
                                            Href = "/api/priorities/" +
priority.PriorityId
                                        }
                                }
                    };
    }
}
```

That class is fairly simple, too. Again, its only role is to map from the model type to the API resource type.

Now let's look at the IHttpPriorityFetcher interface:

```
public interface IHttpPriorityFetcher
{
    Priority GetPriority(long priorityId);
}
```

Andhere's the corresponding implementation:

```
public class HttpPriorityFetcher : IHttpPriorityFetcher
{
    private readonly ISession _session;

    public HttpPriorityFetcher(ISession session)
    {
        _session = session;
    }

    public Priority GetPriority(long priorityId)
    {
        var priority = _session.Get<Priority>(priorityId);
        if (priority == null)
        {
            throw new HttpResponseException(
                new HttpResponseMessage
            {
                        StatusCode = HttpStatusCode.NotFound,
                        ReasonPhrase = string.Format("Priority {0}
not found", priorityId)
            });
        }
        return priority;
    }
}
```

You use this class to fetch the given priority from the database (by priorityId); and then, if it isn't found, the class throws an HTTP-specific exception. When dealing with RESTful services, you want the web requests for resources that don't exist to return a 404 "not found" error. Remember, utilizing REST for the API means that you treat an unknown resource (e.g., Task or Priority) the same as you would an unknown web page on a web site: with a 404 error.

Notice, too, that this implementation includes a more descriptive not found message for the ReasonPhrase property. Normally, when a 404 error is returned, the reason phrase is just "not found"; however, with the task-management service, you want to provide a little more detail, especially since a URL such as /api/tasks/123/categories/456 could technically return a 404 for an unknown task or for an unknown category.

On the PrioritiesController, the two methods are simply named *Get*. As you may recall from Chapter 1 where you were introduced to the Web API, you are taking advantage of the convention-based mechanism for calling controller actions. Basically, if the caller performs an HTTP GET, then the Get method is called. Since the controller has two Get() methods, MVC will call the one with the id argument if the URL used by the caller contains the id segment—per the routes configured in the WebApiConfig.cs file. In other words, when the URL is /api/tasks/123/categories, the Get() method is called. But when the URL is /api/tasks/123/categories/456, the Get(long id) method is called. The same is true for POST, PUT, and DELETE.

The StatusesController, CategoriesController, and UsersController are nearly identical to the PrioritiesController.

The CategoriesController

The biggest difference is that the CategoriesController supports the API's design of allowing the caller to modify the list of categories. Here's what the Post() method looks like:

```
[Authorize(Roles = "Administrators")]
public HttpResponseMessage Post(HttpRequestMessage request, Category category)
{
    var modelCategory = new Data.Model.Category
                        {
                                Description = category.Description,
                                Name = category.Name
                        };

    _session.Save(modelCategory);

    var newCategory = _categoryMapper.CreateCategory(modelCategory);

    var href = newCategory.Links.First(x =>x.Rel == "self").Href;

    var response = request.CreateResponse(HttpStatusCode.Created, newCategory);
    response.Headers.Add("Location", href);

    return response;
}
```

Notice that the method is decorated with the Authorize attribute. Per the API design you did in Chapter 3, you want to restrict modifications to categories to only those callers that belong to the Administrators role.

In the Post() method, the first thing you do is create a new Category model object and set its properties to the incoming category's property values. Next, you use the injected ISession object to save the new category. When using NHibernate, the act of saving an object will automatically set its identity value from the generated value in the database (e.g., the CategoryId).

Once the new category is saved to the database, you use the injected ICategoryMapper object to create an instance of the appropriate resource type, and then grab the new category's self-referencing URL.

Finally, you use the incoming HttpRequestMessage object to generate a response of the new category object—setting the returned HTTP status code to 201: "Created." Next, you set the Location header value to the new category's URL and return the response to the caller. As you may recall from Chapter 3, part of the HTTP protocol is to return the exact URL of any created resources—along with a 201 response code.

For categories, you also want to facilitate a DELETE from the caller—which is also restricted to only Administrators. Here's the code for the DELETE operation:

```
[Authorize(Roles = "Administrators")]
public HttpResponseMessage Delete(long id)
{
    var category = _session.Get<Data.Model.Category>(id);
    if (category!= null)
    {
        _session.Delete(category);
    }

    return new HttpResponseMessage(HttpStatusCode.OK);
}
```

Per HTTP rules, if the resource being deleted doesn't exist, you don't want to generate an error. Instead, you just return 200 "ok" to the caller. Of course, if it does still exist, then you need to delete it, *and then* return 200.

You can examine the task-management service code that accompanies this book to see all of the controller code.

Exploring the Controllers

At this point—provided your solution compiles and runs (if not, consult the sample code that accompanies this book)—you should be able to open your browser and navigate around the REST API. Make sure you've built and published the database project, which includes some test data for categories, priorities, and statuses. The example project also sets the MVC4ServicesBook.Web.Api project's web properties to use IIS Express and the following URL: http://localhost:11000/. If you've configured your solution differently, be sure to adjust the URL appropriately.

To see a list of the task-management service's default categories, use your browser to navigate to http://localhost:11000/api/categories. When prompted for a username and password, use jbob for the username and jbob12345 for the password (provided you used the database project included in the accompanying sample code). This should display an XML document representing the three default categories that were inserted with the ReferenceData.sql script in the database project. Try navigating to the list of statuses and priorities.

Next, try navigating to a specific category. You should be able to take the Href value from one of the Links and paste it into the browser's address bar. For example, if the second category returned with http://localhost:11000/api/categories has a categoryId of 2, then you should be able to navigate to http://localhost:11000/api/categories/2 to see just that specific category. Remember that having a unique address for each resource is a tenet of REST.

Using Fiddler

If you don't already have Fiddler installed on your workstation, download and install it now from www.fiddler2.com/fiddler2/. Once it is installed, fire it up from the Windows Start Menu. Once launched, it will start capturing all of the browser traffic. What you want to do with the tool is to make web requests to the task-management service, similar to what the browser is doing. The difference is that you can create and examine the raw header and body content for request and response messages.

Once you have Fiddler open, go back to your browser and navigate to the categories URL again. Then, back in Fiddler, double-click the 200 response entry in the left-hand panel. Figure 7-1 shows what you should see and double-click.

Figure 7-1. The categories response entry

In the right-hand panel, you should see the request data at the top and the service's response at the bottom. Click the Raw buttons to see both the request and the response. The raw request data should like similar to Figure 7-2.

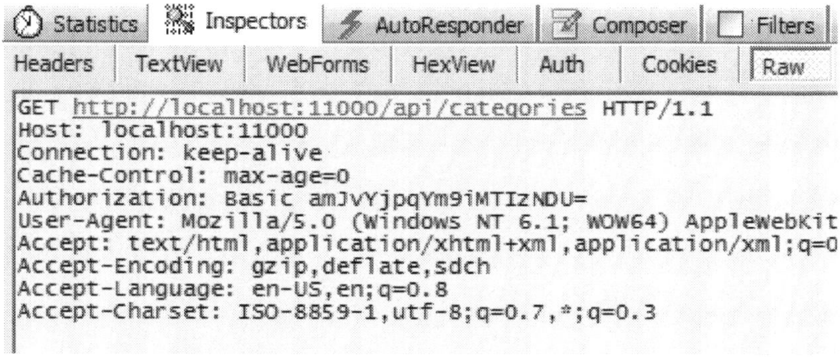

Figure 7-2. The categories raw HTTP request

You should note two things in the request: the URL at the top that represents the GET request URI and the Authorization header value of "Basic amJvYjpqYm9iMTIzNDU=." This is the base64-encoded string of the credentials you entered when the browser prompted you for your username and password.

Now look at the raw data for the HTTP response (the bottom-right panel). Note that it includes an HTTP status code of "200 OK" in the header. Also, the body contains the XML representing all of the categories currently in the database. You can also click the other buttons in the request and response panels to look at the data rendered as XML or just a Headers view. Figure 7-3 shows the response panel just described.

Figure 7-3. *The categories raw response*

To see one of the capabilities of the Web API, click the Composer tab in the top-right request panel. Make sure GET is selected in the dropdown, and then enter the URL to the categories list in the address bar (`http://localhost:11000/api/categories`). Next, enter the following in the Request Headers box:

```
Authorization: Basic amJvYjpqYm9iMTIzNDU=
Content-Length: 41
Host: localhost:11000
```

At this point, the Composer tab should like similar to Figure 7-4.

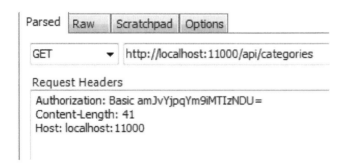

Figure 7-4. *The composer tab for the categories query*

Go ahead and click the Execute button. If all goes well, you should see a new entry in the left-hand panel. Double-click the new entry. On the right-hand side, you can examine the request and response content for your manually composed HTTP request. The response panel should look very similar to Figure 7-3.

Content Negotiation in the Web API

To see the Web API's content negotiation in action, click the Composer tab again, add the following to the Request Headers box, and click Execute:

```
Content-Type: text/xml
```

Double-click the new entry in the left-hand panel, and then notice how the response data is now formatted as XML.

Let's change the Accept header to read this instead (and then click Execute):

```
Content-Type: application/json
```

Notice how the response data is not JSON–formatted text. With the Web API, you get automatic content negotiation! In other words, the caller can specify whether it wants to communicate with XML or communicate with JSON when calling your service. And all you have to do is use the Web API—nothing else is required!

Adding New Resources

Now let's try adding a new category, which will be a POST to the categories URL you've been using. You will need to include the JSON (or XML) of the new category in the request body. First, make sure the Composer tab is selected. Next, make sure that POST is selected in the dropdown (instead of GET). Now enter the following in the Request Headers box:

```
Authorization: Basic amJvYjpqYm9iMTIzNDU=
Content-Length: 41
Host: localhost:11000
Content-Type: application/json
```

In the box labeled Request Body, enter the following JSON text:

```
{"Name":"Project Dirt","Description":"Tasks that belong to project Dirt"}
```

Now click the Execute button to add the new category to the database. This time, when double-clicking the new entry in the left-hand panel, you should see a different type of response that looks similar to Figure 7-5 (when the Raw tab is selected).

```
HTTP/1.1 201 Created
Cache-Control: no-cache
Pragma: no-cache
Content-Type: application/json; charset=utf-8
Expires: -1
Location: /api/categories/4
Server: Microsoft-IIS/8.0
X-AspNet-Version: 4.0.30319
X-SourceFiles: =?UTF-8?B?Qzpcd2RcTXZjNFNlcnZpY2VzQm9v
X-Powered-By: ASP.NET
Date: Mon, 05 Nov 2012 04:40:55 GMT
Content-Length: 167

{"CategoryId":4,"Name":"Project Dirt","Description":"
```

Figure 7-5. *Raw response when adding a new category*

The first thing to note is that the response code is "201 Created." Recall that earlier in this chapter you intentionally returned this particular HTTP response code from the Post() method on the CategoriesController class. You also added a Location header in the response—to represent the new category's URL. If you look closely at the raw response, you should see a Location header value, with the appropriate URL for the new category.

OData Support in the Web API

Another feature of the Web API that you want to explore is its support for OData. This essentially offers the caller the option to specify query-like parameters as part of a URL when calling your service. Provided you have the Microsoft.AspNet.WebApi.OData NuGet package installed (as you did in Chapter 4), all you need to do is return an IQueryable<T> object from a controller method that is decorated with the Queryable attribute. That's it!

Here's what the Get() method looks like on the UsersController:

```
[Queryable]
public IQueryable<Data.Model.User>Get()
{
    return _session.Query<Data.Model.User>();
}
```

By exposing the user data as IQueryable, callers can specify queries similar to the following for the URL (try it in your browser or in Fiddler):

```
/api/users?$filter = Lastname eq 'bob2'
```

The OData protocol supports all kinds of nice query options, including the following:

- `$orderby`
- `$top`
- `$skip`
- `$filter`
- Logical operators
- Grouping
- String functions

At the time of writing, NHibernate didn't support all of the options in the OData specification. But if you want to read more about OData, feel free to browse the official site at `www.odata.org`.

The downside to using the Queryable feature of the Web API is that you must expose your domain model types over the wire. So far, you've been mapping the domain model type over to resource types before returning the data to the caller. But you can't do this if you want to support an OData query interface. This is because the return type of the controller method must be `IQueryable<T>`, and any attempt to map the objects to a different type will force the returned object to be of type `IEnumerable<T>`.

The Task Controllers

In this section of the chapter, you'll look at the task-related controllers of your service.

Separation of Subcontrollers

Subcontrollers are slightly more complicated in that they must provide the resource-addressing capability you specified back in Chapter 3 when you designed the service's API. Each task will have other resources associated with it; namely, it will have a priority, a status, a list of zero or more categories, and a list of zero or more users. Every single resource and every single list of resources hanging off a task must be accessible via a unique URL.

The challenge is to support fetching and updating the data associated with a task, given that the `TasksController` class can only define essentially one `Get()` method, one `Post()` method, and so on. Further, because the URLs were specified as shown in Figure 7-6 (taken from Chapter 3), you need to figure out how to configure the Web API routes so that the resource type names are included in the task URLs.

URI	Verb	Description
/api/tasks	GET	Gets full list of all tasks; optionally specifies a filter.
/api/tasks/123	GET	Gets the details for a single task.
/api/tasks/123/status	GET	Gets just the status information for the specified task.
/api/tasks/123/status/456	PUT	Updates just the status of the specified task.
/api/tasks/123/priority	GET	Gets just the priority information for the specified task.
/api/tasks/123/priority/456	PUT	Updates just the priority of the specified task.
/api/tasks/123/users	GET	Gets the users assigned to the specified task.
/api/tasks/123/users	PUT	Replaces all users on the specified task.
/api/tasks/123/users	DELETE	Deletes all users from the specified task.
/api/tasks/123/users/456	PUT	Adds the specified user (e.g. 456) as an assignee on the task.
/api/tasks/123/users/456	DELETE	Deletes the specified user from the assignee list.
/api/tasks/123/categories	GET	Gets the categories associated with the specified task.
/api/tasks/123/categories	PUT	Replaces all categories on the specified task.
/api/tasks/123/categories	DELETE	Deletes all categories from the specified task.
/api/tasks/123/categories/456	PUT	Adds the specified category (e.g. 456) to the task.
/api/tasks/123/categories/456	DELETE	Removes the specified category from the task.
/api/tasks	POST	Creates a new task.

Figure 7-6. A list of task-related requests

For example, the URL /api/tasks/123 will route to the TasksController.Get(long id) method. But what controller method will the URL /api/tasks/123/status route to? Remember that the method called by MVC/Web API is figured out automatically based on the HTTP request (i.e., the routes don't include GET, POST, PUT, or DELETE).

Task Priority and Status Controllers

The approach used in this book's project addresses this challenge by creating a separate controller for each of the resources associated with a task. This allows you to implement all four HTTP verbs (if needed) on each of the sub-resources that relate to a given task. And in order to make this work properly from the URL, you need to add specific routes for each of those controllers.

Let's start by looking at the routes (as included in the WebApiConfig class):

```
config.Routes.MapHttpRoute(
    name: "TaskStatusApiRoute",
    routeTemplate: "api/tasks/{taskId}/status/{statusId}",
    defaults: new {controller = "TaskStatus", statusId =
RouteParameter.Optional});

config.Routes.MapHttpRoute(
    name: "TaskPriorityApiRoute",
    routeTemplate: "api/tasks/{taskId}/priority/{priorityId}",
    defaults: new {controller = "TaskPriority", priorityId =
RouteParameter.Optional});

config.Routes.MapHttpRoute(
    name: "TaskUsersApiRoute",
    routeTemplate: "api/tasks/{taskId}/users/{userId}",
    defaults: new {controller = "TaskUsers", userId =
RouteParameter.Optional});

config.Routes.MapHttpRoute(
    name: "TaskCategoriesApiRoute",
    routeTemplate: "api/tasks/{taskId}/categories/{categoryId}",
    defaults: new {controller = "TaskCategories", categoryId =
RouteParameter.Optional});
```

Unlike the default route that you saw earlier, these four new routes include the following segments in their URL templates (as specified by the routeTemplate property):

- A hard-coded path to /api/tasks
- A taskID parameter
- A hard-coded path to the appropriate sub-resource (e.g., categories)
- An optional identifier for that particular resource

Also note that each of the routes is mapped to a specific controller, thus allowing the code to respond to all four HTTP verbs for that particular sub-resource. It will help to look at an example of one of these controllers. Here's what the TaskStatusController looks like:

```
[LoggingNHibernateSessions]
public class TaskStatusController : ApiController
{
    private readonly ISession _session;
    private readonly IStatusMapper _statusMapper;
    private readonly IHttpStatusFetcher _statusFetcher;
    private readonly IHttpTaskFetcher _taskFetcher;

    public TaskStatusController(
        IHttpTaskFetcher taskFetcher,
        ISession session,
        IStatusMapper statusMapper,
        IHttpStatusFetcher statusFetcher)
    {
        _taskFetcher = taskFetcher;
        _session = session;
        _statusMapper = statusMapper;
        _statusFetcher = statusFetcher;
    }

    public Status Get(long taskId)
    {
        var task = _taskFetcher.GetTask(taskId);
        return _statusMapper.CreateStatus(task.Status);
    }

    public void Put(long taskId, long statusId)
    {
        var task = _taskFetcher.GetTask(taskId);

        var status = _statusFetcher.GetStatus(statusId);

        task.Status = status;

        _session.Save(task);
    }
}
```

Each of the two controller methods accepts a taskId argument—as specified on the route that belongs to this controller. Also, per the API design, you restrict the caller to only two actions: get a task's status (i.e., the Get() method) and update a task's status (i.e., the Put() method). The same is true for the priority of a task, and so the TaskPriorityController looks almost identical to the TaskStatusController.

The Task Categories and Users Controllers

The controllers for managing a task's categories and users are a bit more complicated, as you're dealing now with lists of resources. As noted in Figure 7-5, you must be able to perform the following actions against a task's categories:

- Get all of the categories associated with a task.

- Replace the entire list of categories for a task.

- Delete all of a task's categories.

- Add a category to a task.

- Delete a category from a task.

This means you should end up with five different methods on the TaskCategoriesController class. Let's look at a couple of them, starting with the PUT method for adding a single category:

```
public void Put(long taskId, long categoryId)
{
    var task = _taskFetcher.GetTask(taskId);

    var category = task.Categories.FirstOrDefault(x => x.CategoryId ==
categoryId);
    if(category!= null)
    {
        return;
    }

    category = _categoryFetcher.GetCategory(categoryId);

    task.Categories.Add(category);

    _session.Save(task);
}
```

In this method, you first fetch the given task. Because you're using an instance of IHttpTaskFetcher, a 404 exception will be thrown and returned to the caller if that particular task doesn't exist. Once you have the task, you can check to see if the given category already belongs to the task; if it does, you simply return it. If not, you need to fetch the category from the database. Again, the IHttpCategoryFetcher will throw a 404 exception if that category doesn't exist. You may recall from Chapter 2's discussion of REST that you need to utilize the standard HTTP response codes in order to have a RESTful service. This means you return a "404 Not Found" status code for resources that don't exist. This is one of the many ways in which REST services differ from RPC-style SOAP services (e.g., a SOAP service for looking up categories would never return a 404 if the caller requested a category that doesn't exist).

After you fetch both the requested task and category, you associate the two, and then save the task object.

Now let's look at the two delete methods. Notice how the first one doesn't take a categoryId, so it will delete all of the categories on the task:

```
public void Delete(long taskId)
{
    var task = _taskFetcher.GetTask(taskId);

    task.Categories
        .ToList()
        .ForEach(x => task.Categories.Remove(x));

    _session.Save(task);
}

public void Delete(long taskId, long categoryId)
{
    var task = _taskFetcher.GetTask(taskId);

    var category = task.Categories.FirstOrDefault(x => x.CategoryId ==
categoryId);
    if (category == null)
    {
        return;
    }

    task.Categories.Remove(category);

    _session.Save(task);
}
```

The TaskUsersController class is similar to the TaskCategoriesController class in that the same five HTTP verbs need to be implemented.

The Task Controller

At last you're ready to look at the TasksController itself. As noted in the previous section, this controller deals only with fetching and updating entire tasks. The other controllers will handle fetching and updating specific status, priority, user, and category data that exists on individual tasks.

Let's look at the TasksController's constructor, as it shows the various mappers being used:

```
public TasksController(
    IHttpTaskFetcher taskFetcher,
    IUserSession userSession,
```

```
        ISession session,
        ICategoryMapper categoryMapper,
        IStatusMapper statusMapper,
        IPriorityMapper priorityMapper,
        IUserMapper userMapper)
    {

        _taskFetcher = taskFetcher;
        _userSession = userSession;
        _session = session;
        _categoryMapper = categoryMapper;
        _statusMapper = statusMapper;
        _priorityMapper = priorityMapper;
        _userMapper = userMapper;
    }
```

The mappers (e.g., ICategoryMapper, IStatusMapper, IPriorityMapper, and IUserMapper) are used to encapsulate the mapping logic that is needed to convert data model objects to service resource objects. For example, the Task.Priority property will contain an instance of MVC4ServicesBook.Data.Model.Priority. However, you need to return an instance of MVC4ServicesBook.Web.Api.Models.Priority to the caller. And since this logic is used in multiple places (and ideally would be unit tested in isolation), it's a great candidate for an injected dependency.

Here are the two Get() methods that exist on the TasksController:

```
public Task Get(long id)
{
    var modelTask = _taskFetcher.GetTask(id);
    var task = CreateTaskFromModel(modelTask);

    return task;
}


public IEnumerable<Task> Get()
{
    var tasks = _session
        .Query<Data.Model.Task>()
        .Where(
            x =>
            x.CreatedBy.UserId == _userSession.UserId || x.Users.
Any(user => user.UserId == _userSession.UserId))
        .Select(CreateTaskFromModel)
        .ToList();

    return tasks;
}
```

```
private Task CreateTaskFromModel(Data.Model.Task modelTask)
{
    var task = new Task
                  {
                      TaskId = modelTask.TaskId,
                      Subject = modelTask.Subject,
                      StartDate = modelTask.StartDate,
                      DateCompleted = modelTask.DateCompleted,
                      DueDate = modelTask.DueDate,
                      CreatedDate = modelTask.CreatedDate,
                      Status = _statusMapper.CreateStatus(modelTask.Status),
                      Priority = _priorityMapper.
CreatePriority(modelTask.Priority),
                      Categories = modelTask
                         .Categories

.Select(_categoryMapper.CreateCategory)
                           .ToList(),
                      Assignees = modelTask
                         .Users
.Select(_userMapper.CreateUser)
                           .ToList()
                  };

    return task;
}
```

Sample Client Code

In this section, you'll see a couple samples for calling the new task-management service. This code is implemented as NUnit tests in a separate project called MVC4ServicesBook.SmokeTests. Each test method simply uses the System.Net.WebClient class for making raw HTTP calls to the service.

Before you look at each test, you need to examine the private method that creates the WebClient instance:

```
private WebClient CreateWebClient()
{
    var webClient = new WebClient();

    const string creds = "jbob"+":"+"jbob12345";
    var bcreds = Encoding.ASCII.GetBytes(creds);
    var base64Creds = Convert.ToBase64String(bcreds);
    webClient.Headers.Add("Authorization", "Basic " + base64Creds);
    return webClient;
}
```

In this method, you first set the Basic authentication credentials to a made-up user (that has already been added to the system via SQL script). Note that the Authorization header uses base64-encoded username and password, separated by a colon.

Let's look first at a GET request to fetch the set of all categories in the system:

```
public const string ApiUrlRoot = "http://localhost:11000/api";

[Test]
public void GetAllCategories()
{
    var client = CreateWebClient();
    var response = client.DownloadString(ApiUrlRoot + "/categories");

    Console.Write(response);
}
```

After you get the client, all you need to do is make a web request with the appropriate URL. By default, the WebClient's DownloadString() method will execute a GET HTTP request. In this test code, all you're doing is writing the response data to the console. Similar code can be used to get all users in the system, by changing the URL to use /users instead of /categories.

The second test method will add a new category to the system using an HTTP POST:

```
[Test]
public void AddNewCategory()
{
    var client = CreateWebClient();

    const string url=ApiUrlRoot+"/categories";
    const string method="POST";
    const string newCategory =
        "{\"Name\":\"Project Red\",\"Description\":\"Tasks that
belong to project Red\"}";

    client.Headers.Add("Content-Type", "application/json");
    var response = client.UploadString(url, method, newCategory);

    Console.Write(response);
}
```

Several bits of code look different in this example. First, you use the WebClient's UploadString() method instead of DownloadString(). This allows you to not only upload the JSON text, but also to set the client's HTTP method. Second, you need to add an HTTP header for Content-Type, which tells the service that the uploaded data is formatted as JSON. If you don't do this, the CategoriesController's Post() method will receive a null Category object—because MVC won't know to parse the data as JSON.

Finally, when calling UploadString(), you need to set the desired HTTP action to POST. Actually, the default action for the UploadString() method is POST. However, it's a good idea to include it in the call to avoid simple mistakes and help make the code clearer to read.

From these two example calls, you should be able to write client code for all other available calls in the task-management service. You only need to adjust the included JSON, URL, and the HTTP method.

Automatic Error Logging

The final section of this chapter will briefly cover error logging as performed from the controller action filter you learned about in Chapter 5—when you were looking at managing the database unit of work and transaction. That same action filter/attribute is a perfect place to put error logging because the filter's OnActionExecuted() method will always execute, even when a controller action generates an exception.

You have two main goals in handling exceptions generated from controller actions:

- Log the error to log4net.
- Return a status code of 500 to the caller, including part of the error message itself.

The second goal is somewhat debatable, as one could argue that you don't want to expose internal error messages to the users. However, it can be much easier to troubleshoot and fix bugs if an accurate error message is returned to the caller or user who will be logging bugs. Further, some messages need to make their way back to the caller. For example, validation errors should certainly be visible to a consumer of the API. A fair approach might be to make this option configurable, and only return the full error messages for certain types of errors or only in certain environments.

You can satisfy both of the goals by using the following code within the LoggingNHibernateSessionAttribute action filter:

```
private void LogException(HttpActionExecutedContext filterContext)
{
    var exception = filterContext.Exception;
    if (exception == null) return;

    var container = GetContainer();
    var logger = container.Get<ILog>();

    logger.Error("Exception occured:", exception);

    var reasonPhrase = GetExceptionMessage(exception);
    if (reasonPhrase.Length > MaxStatusDescriptionLength)
    {
        reasonPhrase = reasonPhrase.Substring(0, MaxStatusDescriptionLength);
    }
```

```
reasonPhrase = reasonPhrase.Replace(Environment.NewLine, " ");

    filterContext.Response = new HttpResponseMessage
                        {
StatusCode = HttpStatusCode.InternalServerError,
                                    ReasonPhrase = reasonPhrase
                        };
}

private string GetExceptionMessage(Exception ex)
{
    var message = ex.Message;
    var innerException = ex.InnerException;
    while (innerException != null)
    {
        message += " -->" + innerException.Message;
        innerException = innerException.InnerException;
    }

    return message;
}
```

First, you check to see if there even is an exception; if there isn't, there is no need to continue. Next, provided you have an exception to handle, you get the logger from the container and log the exception as an error.

The next step is to convert the exception stack to a string—traversing the InnerException tree until you hit bottom. This is implemented in the GetExceptionMessage() method. Next, take that string and make sure it's not too long (anything longer than 512 characters will cause an unhandled exception). Also, remove any end-of-line characters from the string (as that, too, will cause an unhandled exception).

The last step is to set the response to a new HttpResponseMessage object, setting the return code to "500 Internal Server Error." You also set the response's ReasonPhrase to the cleaned-up exception message. Once the MVC has finished executing the action filter/attribute, it will return that specific HttpResponseMessage object to the caller.

All of this is called from within the action filter's OnActionExecuted() method:

```
public override void OnActionExecuted(HttpActionExecutedContext
actionExecutedContext)
{
    EndTransaction(actionExecutedContext);
    CloseSession();
    LogException(actionExecutedContext);

    LogAction(actionExecutedContext.ActionContext.ActionDescriptor,
"EXITING  ");
}
```

Summary

In this chapter, you finally got to build code that let you use the task-management service. Although you didn't specifically walk through every line of code required, you did hit all of the highlights—and you can download the fully functional source code from Apress or from the corresponding GitHub repository at https://github.com/jamiekurtz/Mvc4ServicesBook.

The task-management service is now complete. Moreover, it adheres to the tenets of the REST architecture, taking full advantage of key capabilities within the HTTP protocol. At this point, it should be abundantly clear that a RESTful service is indeed quite a bit different than a SOAP-style service, and that ASP.NET MVC 4 and the Web API provide an excellent platform on which to build such services.

Index